for Music Ministers

Year B • 2021

Katy Beedle Rice

Orin E. Johnson

Verna Holyhead, SGS

with

John R. Donahue, SJ,

Dennis Gunn, CFC,

and John W. Martens

LITURGICAL PRESS

Collegeville, Minnesota

www.litpress.org

Cover design by Monica Bokinskie. Art by Ruberval Monteiro da Silva, OSB.

ISSN 2573-0576

ISBN 978-0-8146-6465-0 978-0-8146-6489-6 (ebook)

ERRATA: LIVING LITURGY™ 2021

Living Liturgy: Spirituality, Celebration, and Catechesis for Sundays and Solemnities (2021) and *Living Liturgy for Music Ministers (2021)* were already at press when Liturgical Press learned of the sexual misconduct allegations against David Haas. Haas's music is recommended in the "About Music" section of these resources on the following days: February 14, April 11, May 2, June 6, and October 3. In support of survivors, we invite communities to disregard these recommendations and pray with the work of other composers.

Multiple song recommendations are offered on February 14, April 11, May 2, and June 6. We hope your community finds inspiration in the other suggested pieces. We offer the following replacement text for the *About Music* section for October 3, 2021:

Love: Music about love should form the core of a parish repertoire this weekend. Consider "Love Goes On" (OCP) by Bernadette Farrell, a paraphrase of the familiar 1 Corinthians reading frequently heard at weddings. "Live On in My Love" from *Psallite* (Liturgical Press) has an accessible tune in litany format. An additional perennial favorite is GIA's "I've Got Peace Like a River," published in the *Lead Me, Guide Me* hymnal.

Liturgical Press has ended the licensure of David Haas's music for inclusion in all publications. Liturgical Press does not own or administer the copyrights of any of Haas's books, music, or published works.

Presented to

____

in grateful appreciation
for your music ministry

____

____
(date)

OURCE

inisters™ is a resource intended to assist ers in their preparation for the liturgy on Sundays and selected solemnities, as well as Ash Wednesday. Included here are reflections on the gospel, and some insight into how the word of God informs daily life. It is hoped that the commentaries and reflections in this resource will assist music ministers with their own personal encounter with the sacred text. Music ministers who have a better understanding of the readings may be more apt to sing with a greater sensitivity to the deeper meaning of God's word.

Living Liturgy for Music Ministers™ has reflections on the gospel readings, brief commentaries connecting the responsorial psalm to the readings, followed by reflections to assist psalmists with preparing for proclamation of the psalms. There are prayers provided for musicians to use with their own spiritual preparation for their ministry. Also included are the readings and responsorial psalms for every Sunday of the liturgical year, as well as for certain solemnities and Ash Wednesday. The second readings are found in an appendix.

This book is an essential resource for music ministers whose own spirituality is nourished by the liturgical cycle and the accompanying Scripture readings, especially the gospel and the psalm. The following outline suggests how this resource might be used by music ministers as they prepare for the liturgical assembly. Of course, adaptations are encouraged as there is no one "right" way to use this book.

On Monday, read only the gospel and reflect on it. Then, read "Reflecting on Living the Gospel" before reading the gospel again. What new insights come to mind? How does the reflection inform your understanding of the sacred text?

On Tuesday, read the first reading. What connections, if any, do you find between it and the gospel? This is a good time to read "Connecting the Responsorial Psalm to the Readings." What new insights come to mind for you? How do these readings inform the situation at your parish, or with your fellow music ministers?

On Wednesday, read the psalm in a prayerful manner. What connections do you draw between the psalm, the gospel, and the first reading? If it is helpful, read the second reading too and let the Scriptures percolate in your spiritual life, with insights bubbling up naturally. When we have been reading God's word, these insights happen not only in prayer but also throughout the week at home, at work, and in daily life.

On Thursday, spend some time with "Ps[illegible] you allow some of the spiritual insights you've gained through prayer inform your proclamation of the psalm?

On Friday, if you haven't already been singing the psalm with your accompanist or fellow ministers, now is a good time to start, at least on your own, or *a cappella*. Use the "Prayer" together as a group or pray it on your own either before or after your practice.

On Saturday and Sunday, spend time in quiet prayer, allowing yourself to be an instrument in God's hands so that the gathered assembly might find meaning and spiritual insight through your ministry. In your prayer allow words or phrases from the gospel, psalm, and first and second readings to come to mind.

Many music ministers find this to be a rich ministry, filled with spirituality and giving new meaning to their daily lives. The personal encounter with the living and sacred text, being the vehicle through which the assembly hears God's word, and the fellowship one experiences throughout the week are sources of consolation and joy. When we minister with the gifts given to us by God, we become who we are meant to be. We actualize the charisms God has bestowed on us, not for our sakes alone, but for the building up of the Christian community. In this way, music ministers live their Christian baptism.

ark 13:3

Jesus said to his disciples: "Be watchful! Be alert! You do not know when the time will come. It is like a man traveling abroad. He leaves home and places his servants in charge, each with his own work, and orders the gatekeeper to be on the watch. Watch, therefore; you do not know when the lord of the house is coming, whether in the evening, or at midnight, or at cockcrow, or in the morning. May he not come suddenly and find you sleeping. What I say to you, I say to all: 'Watch!'"

First Reading **(Isa 63:16b-17, 19b; 64:2-7)**

You, LORD, are our father,
  our redeemer you are named forever.
Why do you let us wander, O LORD, from your ways,
  and harden our hearts so that we fear you not?
Return for the sake of your servants,
  the tribes of your heritage.
Oh, that you would rend the heavens and come down,
  with the mountains quaking before you,
While you wrought awesome deeds we could not hope for,
  such as they had not heard of from of old.
No ear has ever heard, no eye ever seen, any God but you
  doing such deeds for those who wait for him.
Would that you might meet us doing right,
  that we were mindful of you in our ways!
Behold, you are angry, and we are sinful;
  all of us have become like unclean people,
  all our good deeds are like polluted rags;
We have all withered like leaves,
  and our guilt carries us away like the wind.
There is none who calls upon your name,
  who rouses himself to cling to you;
For you have hidden your face from us
  and have delivered us up to our guilt.

Yet, O LORD, you are our father;
we are the clay and you the potter:
we are all the work of your hands.

***Responsorial Psalm* (Ps 80:2-3, 15-16, 18-19)**

℞. (4) Lord, make us turn to you; let us see your face and we shall be saved.

O shepherd of Israel, hearken,
from your throne upon the cherubim, shine forth.
Rouse your power,
and come to save us.

℞. Lord, make us turn to you; let us see your face and we shall be saved.

Once again, O LORD of hosts,
look down from heaven, and see;
take care of this vine,
and protect what your right hand has planted,
the son of man whom you yourself made strong.

℞. Lord, make us turn to you; let us see your face and we shall be saved.

May your help be with the man of your right hand,
with the son of man whom you yourself made strong.
Then we will no more withdraw from you;
give us new life, and we will call upon your name.

℞. Lord, make us turn to you; let us see your face and we shall be saved.

See Appendix, p. 199, for Second Reading

Reflecting on Living the Gospel

"Be watchful! Be alert!" are the first words with which Mark greets us at the beginning of this new year of the church. They are also the last words spoken by Jesus in Mark's gospel (Mark 13:37) before the vortex of violence begins to suck Jesus into the passion and death that he will conquer by his resurrection. So even as we begin Advent, we are reminded of the paschal mystery of Christ, the hub of the liturgical year.

Connecting the Responsorial Psalm to the Readings

Today's psalm matches the first reading in urgency and tone. The psalmist pleads with God to "[r]ouse your power, / and come to save us." In the gospel, Jesus calls his disciples to "[b]e watchful! Be alert!" But in the psalm, God is the one who is called upon to "hearken" to the cries of his people and to "look down from heaven, and see." In the covenant, God, with consideration and patience, waits for our full and wholehearted response to his invitation to relationship. We are not forced, and at times it can seem as if God is far away, even when we know he is closer than our very breath.

Psalmist Preparation

In your life of faith, when have you been most in need of God's strength and saving power?

Prayer

Patient God, ever abounding in mercy,
grant us the courage and confidence, during this season of anxious anticipation,
to respond to your call to *turn to you; let us see your face and we shall be saved.*
For you, with Son and Spirit, are one God, forever and ever. Amen.

DECEMBER 6, 2020

***Gospel* (Mark 1:1-8; L5B)**

The beginning of the gospel of Jesus Christ the Son of God.
As it is written in Isaiah the prophet:
Behold, I am sending my messenger
ahead of you;
he will prepare your way.
A voice of one crying out in the desert:
"Prepare the way of the Lord,
make straight his paths."
John the Baptist appeared in the desert proclaiming a baptism of repentance for the forgiveness of sins. People of the whole Judean countryside and all the inhabitants of Jerusalem were going out to him and were being baptized by him in the Jordan River as they acknowledged their sins. John was clothed in camel's hair, with a leather belt around his waist. He fed on locusts and wild honey. And this is what he proclaimed: "One mightier than I is coming after me. I am not worthy to stoop and loosen the thongs of his sandals. I have baptized you with water; he will baptize you with the Holy Spirit."

***First Reading* (Isa 40:1-5, 9-11)**

Comfort, give comfort to my people,
says your God.
Speak tenderly to Jerusalem, and proclaim to her
that her service is at an end,
her guilt is expiated;
Indeed, she has received from the hand of the LORD
double for all her sins.

A voice cries out:
In the desert prepare the way of the LORD!
Make straight in the wasteland a highway for our God!
Every valley shall be filled in,
every mountain and hill shall be made low;
The rugged land shall be made a plain,
the rough country, a broad valley.
Then the glory of the LORD shall be revealed,
and all people shall see it together;
for the mouth of the LORD has spoken.

Go up on to a high mountain,
  Zion, herald of glad tidings;
Cry out at the top of your voice,
  Jerusalem, herald of good news!
Fear not to cry out
  and say to the cities of Judah:
  Here is your God!
Here comes with power
  the Lord GOD,
  who rules by his strong arm;
Here is his reward with him,
  his recompense before him.
Like a shepherd he feeds his flock;
  in his arms he gathers the lambs,
Carrying them in his bosom,
  and leading the ewes with care.

***Responsorial Psalm* (Ps 85:9-10, 11-12, 13-14)**

℟. (8) Lord, let us see your kindness, and grant us your salvation.

I will hear what God proclaims;
  the LORD—for he proclaims peace to his people.
Near indeed is his salvation to those who fear him,
  glory dwelling in our land.

℟. Lord, let us see your kindness, and grant us your salvation.

Kindness and truth shall meet;
  justice and peace shall kiss.
Truth shall spring out of the earth,
  and justice shall look down from heaven.

℟. Lord, let us see your kindness, and grant us your salvation.

The LORD himself will give his benefits;
  our land shall yield its increase.
Justice shall walk before him,
  and prepare the way of his steps.

℟. Lord, let us see your kindness, and grant us your salvation.

See Appendix, p. 199, for Second Reading

Reflecting on Living the Gospel

The Liturgy of the Word puts the adult John before us today and next Sunday to block our view of "baby Jesus," and so remind us that the Advent–Christmas mystery is less about the child and more about the adult Coming One and the mystery of his life, death, and resurrection that he offers to us as our own mystery. We are called to make our way down to the Jordan with the hopeful and curious crowds to see this wilderness man.

Connecting the Responsorial Psalm to the Readings

Our psalm response implores the Lord, "[L]et us see your kindness, and grant us your salvation." The kindness of the Lord is on display in each of today's readings. The prophet Isaiah proclaims a forgiving God, ready to save his captive people and return them to their homeland. In the second reading, kindness can be read into the very "delay" that has caused some to doubt Jesus's return. For those who require more time to come to repentance, God has allowed for an extended period of waiting for the day of the Lord. And in the gospel, God, in his goodness, sends a messenger, John the Baptist, to prepare the people to recognize Jesus when he comes to minister among them.

Psalmist Preparation

In our own lives, the kindness of God surrounds and sustains us. The kindness of our Creator calls us to live lives that reflect God's glory and proclaim "peace to his people." How have you experienced God's kindness recently?

Prayer

Merciful God,
you are present always and always love.
Make us ever mindful of your presence and your presence to those around us each day.
Lord, let us see your kindness, and grant us your salvation.
Through your coming Son, Christ our Lord and Messiah. Amen.

THE IMMACULATE CONCEPTION OF THE BLESSED VIRGIN MARY

***Gospel* (Luke 1:26-38; L689)**

The angel Gabriel was sent from God to a town of Galilee called Nazareth, to a virgin betrothed to a man named Joseph, of the house of David, and the virgin's name was Mary. And coming to her, he said, "Hail, full of grace! The Lord is with you." But she was greatly troubled at what was said and pondered what sort of greeting this might be. Then the angel said to her, "Do not be afraid, Mary, for you have found favor with God. Behold, you will conceive in your womb and bear a son, and you shall name him Jesus. He will be great and will be called Son of the Most High, and the Lord God will give him the throne of David his father, and he will rule over the house of Jacob forever, and of his Kingdom there will be no end." But Mary said to the angel, "How can this be, since I have no relations with a man?" And the angel said to her in reply, "The Holy Spirit will come upon you, and the power of the Most High will overshadow you. Therefore the child to be born will be called holy, the Son of God. And behold, Elizabeth, your relative, has also conceived a son in her old age, and this is the sixth month for her who was called barren; for nothing will be impossible for God." Mary said, "Behold, I am the handmaid of the Lord. May it be done to me according to your word." Then the angel departed from her.

***First Reading* (Gen 3:9-15, 20)**

After the man, Adam, had eaten of the tree, the LORD God called to the man and asked him, "Where are you?" He answered, "I heard you in the garden; but I was afraid, because I was naked, so I hid myself." Then he asked, "Who told you that you were naked? You have eaten, then, from the tree of which I had forbidden you to eat!" The man replied, "The woman whom you put here with me— she gave me fruit from the tree, and so I ate it." The LORD God then asked the woman, "Why did you do such a thing?" The woman answered, "The serpent tricked me into it, so I ate it."

Then the LORD God said to the serpent:

"Because you have done this, you shall be banned
from all the animals
and from all the wild creatures;
on your belly shall you crawl,
and dirt shall you eat
all the days of your life.
I will put enmity between you and the woman,
and between your offspring and hers;
he will strike at your head,
while you strike at his heel."

The man called his wife Eve, because she became the mother of all the living.

Responsorial Psalm **(Ps 98:1, 2-3, 3-4)**

℟. (1a) Sing to the Lord a new song, for he has done marvelous deeds.

Sing to the LORD a new song,
for he has done wondrous deeds;
his right hand has won victory for him,
his holy arm.

℟. Sing to the Lord a new song, for he has done marvelous deeds.

The LORD has made his salvation known:
in the sight of the nations he has revealed his justice.
He has remembered his kindness and his faithfulness
toward the house of Israel.

℟. Sing to the Lord a new song, for he has done marvelous deeds.

All the ends of the earth have seen
the salvation by our God.
Sing joyfully to the LORD, all you lands;
break into song; sing praise.

℟. Sing to the Lord a new song, for he has done marvelous deeds.

See Appendix, p. 199, for Second Reading

THE IMMACULATE CONCEPTION OF THE BLESSED VIRGIN MARY

Reflecting on Living the Gospel

The teaching of Mary's immaculate conception developed in the living tradition of the church as it reflected on the holiness necessary for the task to which she had been called. We should continue to reflect on Mary's holiness, too, for it was through her being prepared to receive the Son of God that the Second Person of the Trinity became incarnate. It was necessary that she be "full of grace," free from all stain of sin, so that all the world could encounter the Word in the flesh.

Connecting the Responsorial Psalm to the Readings

On today's feast we proclaim, "Sing to the Lord a new song, for he has done marvelous deeds." Today's gospel combines the miraculous with the ordinary. A woman discovers she is going to have a baby, an event that happens every day all over the world. While the advent of any new life calls us to marvel at creativity of our God, the child that is conceived in Mary's womb by the power of the Holy Spirit is born not only to her but to all of us for he is "holy, the Son of God."

Psalmist Preparation

The child born to this immaculate mother calls all of us to newness of life. In this season of Advent waiting and preparation, how are you being called to renewal and transformation?

Prayer

Ineffable Creator,
the mystery of who you are is great; the essence of who you are is simple: love.
Like Mary, who knew this well, help us to respond "yes" to your calls,
and sing to you *a new song* as you continue to do *marvelous deeds* in our lives. Amen.

DECEMBER 13, 2020

***Gospel* (John 1:6-8, 19-28; L8B)**

A man named John was sent from God. He came for testimony, to testify to the light, so that all might believe through him. He was not the light, but came to testify to the light.

And this is the testimony of John. When the Jews from Jerusalem sent priests and Levites to him to ask him, "Who are you?" he admitted and did not deny it, but admitted, "I am not the Christ." So they asked him, "What are you then? Are you Elijah?" And he said, "I am not." "Are you the Prophet?" He answered, "No." So they said to him, "Who are you, so we can give an answer to those who sent us? What do you have to say for yourself?" He said:

"I am *the voice of one crying out in the*
desert,
'make straight the way of the Lord,'

as Isaiah the prophet said." Some Pharisees were also sent. They asked him, "Why then do you baptize if you are not the Christ or Elijah or the Prophet?" John answered them, "I baptize with water; but there is one among you whom you do not recognize, the one who is coming after me, whose sandal strap I am not worthy to untie." This happened in Bethany across the Jordan, where John was baptizing.

***First Reading* (Isa 61:1-2a, 10-11)**

The spirit of the Lord GOD is upon me,
because the LORD has anointed me;
He has sent me to bring glad tidings to the poor,
to heal the brokenhearted,
To proclaim liberty to the captives
and release to the prisoners,
To announce a year of favor from the LORD
and a day of vindication by our God.

I rejoice heartily in the LORD,
in my God is the joy of my soul;

For he has clothed me with a robe of salvation
and wrapped me in a mantle of justice,
Like a bridegroom adorned with a diadem,
like a bride bedecked with her jewels.
As the earth brings forth its plants,
and a garden makes its growth spring up,
So will the Lord God make justice and praise
spring up before all the nations.

***Responsorial Psalm* (Luke 1:46-48, 49-50, 53-54)**

℟. (Isa 61:10b) My soul rejoices in my God.

My soul proclaims the greatness of the Lord;
my spirit rejoices in God my Savior,
for he has looked upon his lowly servant.
From this day all generations will call me blessed:

℟. My soul rejoices in my God.

The Almighty has done great things for me,
and holy is his Name.
He has mercy on those who fear him
in every generation.

℟. My soul rejoices in my God.

He has filled the hungry with good things,
and the rich he has sent away empty.
He has come to the help of his servant Israel
for he has remembered his promise of mercy.

℟. My soul rejoices in my God.

See Appendix, p. 200, for Second Reading

Reflecting on Living the Gospel

John identifies himself not as the Messiah, but as the fulfillment of long-ago prophecies, as the one who prepares the way for the coming Messiah. But the questions still remained, even for John. Who ever thought that it would happen through a young, unmarried woman, that God would look "with favor on the lowliness of his servant," Mary? God asks that as we wait for fulfillment, we be prepared for God to do new things, unexpected things, and be ready for the unlikeliest of answers.

Connecting the Responsorial Psalm to the Readings

For Gaudete (Latin for "Rejoice") Sunday, our "psalm" comes from Mary's own song of praise to her Creator, the *Magnificat*. In the first reading, the responsorial psalm, and the second reading we find today's theme of joy expounded upon. The prophet Isaiah proclaims, "I rejoice heartily in the Lord, / in my God is the joy of my soul." Mary responds to Elizabeth's claim that Mary herself is "blessed" by singling out the source of all blessing: "My soul proclaims the greatness of the Lord; / my spirit rejoices in God my savior." And St. Paul exhorts the Thessalonians to "[r]ejoice always." Our readings leave no doubt that joy is a central part of any Christian's life and not an optional attitude to be adopted only when we are naturally inclined to happiness.

Psalmist Preparation

As you prepare to lead the assembly in praying Mary's treasured words, pause to consider the place of joy in your own faith journey. How do you strive to embody this joy in your ministry and in your daily life?

Prayer

God of life and living God,
it is you who bring joy and vitality to all.
Grant us eyes of faith to see you and your bliss all around us.
May we ever be able to say to you, *My soul rejoices in my God.* Amen.

***Gospel* (Luke 1:26-38; L11B)**

The angel Gabriel was sent from God to a town of Galilee called Nazareth, to a virgin betrothed to a man named Joseph, of the house of David, and the virgin's name was Mary. And coming to her, he said, "Hail, full of grace! The Lord is with you." But she was greatly troubled at what was said and pondered what sort of greeting this might be. Then the angel said to her, "Do not be afraid, Mary, for you have found favor with God.

"Behold, you will conceive in your womb and bear a son, and you shall name him Jesus. He will be great and will be called Son of the Most High, and the Lord God will give him the throne of David his father, and he will rule over the house of Jacob forever, and of his kingdom there will be no end." But Mary said to the angel, "How can this be, since I have no relations with a man?" And the angel said to her in reply, "The Holy Spirit will come upon you, and the power of the Most High will overshadow you. Therefore the child to be born will be called holy, the Son of God. And behold, Elizabeth, your relative, has also conceived a son in her old age, and this is the sixth month for her who was called barren; for nothing will be impossible for God." Mary said, "Behold, I am the handmaid of the Lord. May it be done to me according to your word." Then the angel departed from her.

***First Reading* (2 Sam 7:1-5, 8b-12, 14a, 16)**

When King David was settled in his palace, and the LORD had given him rest from his enemies on every side, he said to Nathan the prophet, "Here I am living in a house of cedar, while the ark of God dwells in a tent!" Nathan answered the king, "Go, do whatever you have in mind, for the LORD is with you." But that night the LORD spoke to Nathan and said: "Go, tell my servant David, 'Thus says the LORD: Should you build me a house to dwell in?

"'It was I who took you from the pasture and from the care of the flock to be commander of my people Israel. I have been with you wherever you went, and I have destroyed all your enemies before you. And I will make you famous like the great ones of the earth. I will fix a place for my people Israel; I will plant them so that they may dwell in their place without further disturbance. Neither shall the wicked continue to afflict them as they did of old, since the time I first appointed judges over my people Israel. I will give you rest from all your enemies. The LORD also reveals to you that he will establish a house for you. And when your time comes and you rest with your ancestors, I will raise up your heir after you, sprung from your loins, and I will make his kingdom firm. I will be a father to him, and he shall be a son to me. Your house and your kingdom shall endure forever before me; your throne shall stand firm forever.'"

***Responsorial Psalm* (Ps 89:2-3, 4-5, 27, 29)**

℟. (2a) For ever I will sing the goodness of the Lord.

The promises of the LORD I will sing forever;
through all generations my mouth shall proclaim your faithfulness.
For you have said, "My kindness is established forever";
in heaven you have confirmed your faithfulness.

℟. For ever I will sing the goodness of the Lord.

"I have made a covenant with my chosen one,
I have sworn to David my servant:
Forever will I confirm your posterity
and establish your throne for all generations."

℟. For ever I will sing the goodness of the Lord.

"He shall say of me, 'You are my father,
my God, the Rock, my savior.'
Forever I will maintain my kindness toward him,
and my covenant with him stands firm."

℟. For ever I will sing the goodness of the Lord.

See Appendix, p. 200, for Second Reading

Reflecting on Living the Gospel

As we light the last of the four candles of our Advent wreath, it is up to us, disciples of the Light of the world, to catch fire from Christ's mystery and bring something of this fire and light into our own lives and, especially, into the lives of those for whom Christmas may not be a feast of joy but a time of darkness. May the fire we catch from Christ be our readiness to be consumed like him in the flame of loving service of our sisters and brothers.

Connecting the Responsorial Psalm to the Readings

Today's psalm seems to convey joy, praise, and thanksgiving, so it might be surprising to discover it is titled as "[a] Lament over God's Promise to David" in the *New American Bible Revised Edition*. Many verses after the ones proclaimed today found the reason for lamentation: "But now you have rejected and spurned, / been enraged at your anointed. . . . You have exalted the right hand of his foes, / have gladdened all his enemies" (vv. 39, 43; NABRE). It is noteworthy that the words of praise and trust that we pray today were first sung in the context of defeat rather than victory. It is one thing to praise God in times of peace and abundance, and quite another to say, "For ever I will sing the goodness of the Lord" when facing ruin and uncertainty. Perhaps this is the only kind of faith strong enough to span from one generation to another.

Psalmist Preparation

In preparing to cantor today's psalm, how does it change your understanding of the words to know that it was first sung in a time of sorrow and looming despair? Where, within your community or within the wider world, is the hope of the psalmist most needed?

Prayer

Creator of all,
there is nothing you have made which is not beautiful.
As the coming of your son draws near,
make us mindful of the magnificence of your handiwork,
that we may forever *sing the goodness of the Lord,*
echoing your artistry and creativity. Amen.

DECEMBER 25, 2020

***Gospel* (Matt 1:1-25 [or 1:18-25]; L13ABC)**

The book of the genealogy of Jesus Christ, the son of David, the son of Abraham.

Abraham became the father of Isaac, Isaac the father of Jacob, Jacob the father of Judah and his brothers. Judah became the father of Perez and Zerah, whose mother was Tamar. Perez became the father of Hezron, Hezron the father of Ram, Ram the father of Amminadab. Amminadab became the father of Nahshon, Nahshon the father of Salmon, Salmon the father of Boaz, whose mother was Rahab. Boaz became the father of Obed, whose mother was Ruth. Obed became the father of Jesse, Jesse the father of David the king.

David became the father of Solomon, whose mother had been the wife of Uriah. Solomon became the father of Rehoboam, Rehoboam the father of Abijah, Abijah the father of Asaph. Asaph became the father of Jehoshaphat, Jehoshaphat the father of Joram, Joram the father of Uzziah. Uzziah became the father of Jotham, Jotham the father of Ahaz, Ahaz the father of Hezekiah. Hezekiah became the father of Manasseh, Manasseh the father of Amos, Amos the father of Josiah. Josiah became the father of Jechoniah and his brothers at the time of the Babylonian exile.

After the Babylonian exile, Jechoniah became the father of Shealtiel, Shealtiel the father of Zerubbabel, Zerubbabel the father of Abiud. Abiud became the father of Eliakim, Eliakim the father of Azor, Azor the father of Zadok. Zadok became the father of Achim, Achim the father of Eliud, Eliud the father of Eleazar. Eleazar became the father of Matthan, Matthan the father of Jacob, Jacob the father of Joseph, the husband of Mary. Of her was born Jesus who is called the Christ.

Thus the total number of generations from Abraham to David is fourteen generations; from David to the Babylonian exile, fourteen generations; from the Babylonian exile to the Christ, fourteen generations.

Now this is how the birth of Jesus Christ came about. When his mother Mary was betrothed to Joseph, but before they lived together, she was found with child through the Holy Spirit. Joseph her husband, since he was a righteous man, yet unwilling to expose her to shame, decided to divorce her quietly. Such was his intention when, behold, the angel of the Lord appeared to him in a dream and said, "Joseph, son of David, do not be afraid to take Mary your wife into your home. For it is through the Holy Spirit that this child has been conceived in her. She will bear a son and you are to name him Jesus, because he will save his people from their sins." All this took place to fulfill what the Lord had said through the prophet:

Behold, the virgin shall conceive and bear a son,
and they shall name him Emmanuel,

which means "God is with us." When Joseph awoke, he did as the angel of the Lord had commanded him and took his wife into his home. He had no relations with her until she bore a son, and he named him Jesus.

***First Reading* (Isa 62:1-5)**

For Zion's sake I will not be silent,
for Jerusalem's sake I will not be quiet,
until her vindication shines forth like the dawn
and her victory like a burning torch.

Nations shall behold your vindication,
and all the kings your glory;
you shall be called by a new name
pronounced by the mouth of the LORD.
You shall be a glorious crown in the hand of the LORD,
a royal diadem held by your God.
No more shall people call you "Forsaken,"
or your land "Desolate,"
but you shall be called "My Delight,"
and your land "Espoused."
For the LORD delights in you
and makes your land his spouse.
As a young man marries a virgin,
your Builder shall marry you;
and as a bridegroom rejoices in his bride
so shall your God rejoice in you.

***Responsorial Psalm* (Ps 89:4-5, 16-17, 27, 29)**

℟. (2a) For ever I will sing the goodness of the Lord.

I have made a covenant with my chosen one,
I have sworn to David my servant:
forever will I confirm your posterity
and establish your throne for all generations.

℟. For ever I will sing the goodness of the Lord.

Blessed the people who know the joyful shout;
in the light of your countenance, O LORD, they walk.
At your name they rejoice all the day,
and through your justice they are exalted.

℟. For ever I will sing the goodness of the Lord.

He shall say of me, "You are my father,
my God, the rock, my savior."
Forever I will maintain my kindness toward him,
and my covenant with him stands firm.

℟. For ever I will sing the goodness of the Lord.

See Appendix, p. 200, for Second Reading

Reflecting on Living the Gospel

Matthew's beginning does not limit itself to Jesus's origins, his genealogy, and manner of conception. It is truly concerned with the Gospel, that is, with the good news given to the community that Matthew is addressing. Jesus is the summit toward which past sacred history converges, as does our history, which begins with his birth. From beginning to end, this history is lived out by men and women from generation to generation. It is the duty of each of us to find our proper place in it.

Connecting the Responsorial Psalm to the Readings

Today's gospel begins with the "genealogy of Jesus Christ." Matthew records forty-two generations from Abraham to Jesus and while most of these names might be unfamiliar to us, we know that each generation in its own time and way sang of "the goodness of the Lord" so that when the time was right Emmanuel, God in the flesh, would be recognized by peasants, shepherds, and kings.

THE NATIVITY OF THE LORD
Vigil Mass

Psalmist Preparation

Now this song has been entrusted to us. We are the blessed ones who "know the joyful shout." This Christmas, how will you recommit your life to being a song of praise to God?

Prayer

God, our rock and savior,
through all generations you are covenant,
through all generations you are holy.
Forever I will sing the goodness that you are,
and proclaim with shouts of joy
your salvation, freely given, available to all. Amen.

DECEMBER 25, 2020

Gospel **(Luke 2:1-14; L14ABC)**

In those days a decree went out from Caesar Augustus that the whole world should be enrolled. This was the first enrollment, when Quirinius was governor of Syria. So all went to be enrolled, each to his own town. And Joseph too went up from Galilee from the town of Nazareth to Judea, to the city of David that is called Bethlehem, because he was of the house and family of David, to be enrolled with Mary, his betrothed, who was with child. While they were there, the time came for her to have her child, and she gave birth to her firstborn son. She wrapped him in swaddling clothes and laid him in a manger, because there was no room for them in the inn.

Now there were shepherds in that region living in the fields and keeping the night watch over their flock. The angel of the Lord appeared to them and the glory of the Lord shone around them, and they were struck with great fear. The angel said to them, "Do not be afraid; for behold, I proclaim to you good news of great joy that will be for all the people. For today in the city of David a savior has been born for you who is Christ and Lord. And this will be a sign for you: you will find an infant wrapped in swaddling clothes and lying in a manger." And suddenly there was a multitude of the heavenly host with the angel, praising God and saying:

"Glory to God in the highest
and on earth peace to those on whom his favor rests."

First Reading **(Isa 9:1-6)**

The people who walked in darkness
have seen a great light;
upon those who dwelt in the land of gloom
a light has shone.
You have brought them abundant joy
and great rejoicing,
as they rejoice before you as at the harvest,
as people make merry when dividing spoils.
For the yoke that burdened them,
the pole on their shoulder,
and the rod of their taskmaster
you have smashed, as on the day of Midian.
For every boot that tramped in battle,
every cloak rolled in blood,
will be burned as fuel for flames.

For a child is born to us, a son is given us;
upon his shoulder dominion rests.
They name him Wonder-Counselor, God-Hero,
Father-Forever, Prince of Peace.
His dominion is vast
and forever peaceful,
from David's throne, and over his kingdom,
which he confirms and sustains
by judgment and justice,
both now and forever.
The zeal of the LORD of hosts will do this!

Responsorial Psalm **(Ps 96:1-2, 2-3, 11-12, 13)**

℟. (Luke 2:11) Today is born our Savior, Christ the Lord.

Sing to the LORD a new song;
sing to the LORD, all you lands.
Sing to the LORD; bless his name.

℟. Today is born our Savior, Christ the Lord.

Announce his salvation, day after day.
Tell his glory among the nations;
among all peoples, his wondrous deeds.

℟. Today is born our Savior, Christ the Lord.

Let the heavens be glad and the earth rejoice;
let the sea and what fills it resound;
let the plains be joyful and all that is in them!
Then shall all the trees of the forest exult.

℟. Today is born our Savior, Christ the Lord.

They shall exult before the LORD, for he comes;
for he comes to rule the earth.
He shall rule the world with justice
and the peoples with his constancy.

℟. Today is born our Savior, Christ the Lord.

See Appendix, p. 200, for Second Reading

Reflecting on Living the Gospel

The beauty of Luke's narrative reminds us that through the incarnation, the human condition is now suffused with God's beauty. Still, the contemporary marketing of Christmas can mask the stark reality of Jesus's birth. Luke used the same term for the "inn" (Luke 2:7) that did not welcome Mary and Joseph and for the "guest room" (Luke 22:11, *katalyma*) where Jesus celebrates his final supper and speaks of his body, which will be given and his blood shed. The shadow of the cross falls even upon the crèche of Bethlehem.

Connecting the Responsorial Psalm to the Readings

This night's psalm response is taken from the proclamation made by the angel in today's gospel. Speaking to the frightened shepherds, with glory streaming forth, the angel says, "Do not be afraid; / for behold, I proclaim to you good news of great joy / that will be for all people. / For today in the city of David / a savior has been born for you who is Christ and Lord." Not only for the shepherds, this "good news of great joy" is for us, here and now. This event that took place thousands of years ago in the town of Bethlehem is taken from history so that we might live it anew as we proclaim, "Today is born our Savior, Christ the Lord."

Psalmist Preparation

After hearing the angel's proclamation, the shepherds' lives were most likely changed forever. How does the good news of this child's birth bring about ongoing transformation in your own life?

Prayer

Most Blessed God,
both heaven and earth *sing* your praises
and exult your most holy name.
A great redeemer has been given us,
your son of *justice*, mercy, and truth.
Constant is your love for us, and eternal your salvation.
By your incarnation you invite us to be with you, one day, in glory.
You are wonderful, you are *Lord*. Amen.

***Gospel* (Luke 2:15-20; L15ABC)**

When the angels went away from them to heaven, the shepherds said to one another, "Let us go, then, to Bethlehem to see this thing that has taken place, which the Lord has made known to us." So they went in haste and found Mary and Joseph, and the infant lying in the manger. When they saw this, they made known the message that had been told them about this child. All who heard it were amazed by what had been told them by the shepherds. And Mary kept all these things, reflecting on them in her heart. Then the shepherds returned, glorifying and praising God for all they had heard and seen, just as it had been told to them.

***First Reading* (Isa 62:11-12)**

See, the LORD proclaims
 to the ends of the earth:
say to daughter Zion,
 your savior comes!
Here is his reward with him,
 his recompense before him.
They shall be called the holy people,
 the redeemed of the LORD,
and you shall be called "Frequented,"
 a city that is not forsaken.

***Responsorial Psalm* (Ps 97:1, 6, 11-12)**

℟. A light will shine on us this day: the Lord is born for us.

The LORD is king; let the earth rejoice;
 let the many isles be glad.
The heavens proclaim his justice,
 and all peoples see his glory.

℟. A light will shine on us this day: the Lord is born for us.

Light dawns for the just;
 and gladness, for the upright of heart.
Be glad in the LORD, you just,
 and give thanks to his holy name.

℟. A light will shine on us this day: the Lord is born for us.

See Appendix, p. 201, for Second Reading

Reflecting on Living the Gospel

Mary "kept all these things, reflecting on them in her heart." Doubtless, she did not at first perceive the full depth and meaning of her experience. Mary followed and meditated on the various phases of the mystery of her son's life. Though unique, this itinerary of the "privileged of God" maps out the road that all believers must follow. Everyone, including Mary, enters gradually into this mystery. Faith is nourished by listening to Scripture and by meditating on all the events in which God comes to us.

Connecting the Responsorial Psalm to the Readings

This morning's gospel begins, "When the angels went away from them to heaven . . ." We could imagine the shepherds transitioning from the glory of heavenly light in the angels' presence to the darkness of a winter night. But they are not perturbed and instead with excitement run through the gloom to find the one who will later proclaim, "I am the light of the world" (John 8:12; NABRE) waiting for them in a manger. Our psalm response sings of this child who fulfills Isaiah's prophecy that "the people who walked in darkness have seen a great light" (Isa 9:1; NABRE) and we proclaim, "A light will shine on us this day: the Lord is born for us."

Psalmist Preparation

How are you being called to welcome the light of the Lord into places of darkness within your own life?

Prayer

Incarnate God,
no longer distant and fearful,
now near us, with us, full of love and hope,
help us, like Joseph and Mary, to welcome you into our homes.
Make us aware of the divine mysteries of this day,
always *reflecting on them* in our hearts. Amen.

Gospel (John 1:1-18 [or 1:1-5, 9-14]; L16ABC)

In the beginning was the Word,
and the Word was with God,
and the Word was God.
He was in the beginning with God.
All things came to be through him,
and without him nothing came to be.
What came to be through him was life,
and this life was the light of the human race;
the light shines in the darkness,
and the darkness has not overcome it.

A man named John was sent from God. He came for testimony, to testify to the light, so that all might believe through him. He was not the light, but came to testify to the light. The true light, which enlightens everyone, was coming into the world.

He was in the world,
and the world came to be through him,
but the world did not know him.
He came to what was his own,
but his own people did not accept him.

But to those who did accept him he gave power to become children of God, to those who believe in his name, who were born not by natural generation nor by human choice nor by a man's decision but of God.

And the Word became flesh
and made his dwelling among us,
and we saw his glory,
the glory as of the Father's only Son,
full of grace and truth.

John testified to him and cried out, saying, "This was he of whom I said, 'The one who is coming after me ranks ahead of me because he existed before me.'" From his fullness we have all received, grace in place of grace, because while the law was given through Moses, grace and truth came through Jesus Christ. No one has ever seen God. The only Son, God, who is at the Father's side, has revealed him.

***First Reading* (Isa 52:7-10)**

How beautiful upon the mountains
  are the feet of him who brings glad tidings,
announcing peace, bearing good news,
  announcing salvation, and saying to Zion,
  "Your God is King!"

Hark! Your sentinels raise a cry,
  together they shout for joy,
for they see directly, before their eyes,
  the LORD restoring Zion.
Break out together in song,
  O ruins of Jerusalem!
For the LORD comforts his people,
  he redeems Jerusalem.
The LORD has bared his holy arm
  in the sight of all the nations;
all the ends of the earth will behold
  the salvation of our God.

***Responsorial Psalm* (Ps 98:1, 2-3, 3-4, 5-6)**

℟. (3c) All the ends of the earth have seen the saving power of God.

Sing to the LORD a new song,
  for he has done wondrous deeds;
his right hand has won victory for him,
  his holy arm.

℟. All the ends of the earth have seen the saving power of God.

The LORD has made his salvation known:
  in the sight of the nations he has revealed his justice.
He has remembered his kindness and his faithfulness
  toward the house of Israel.

℟. All the ends of the earth have seen the saving power of God.

All the ends of the earth have seen
  the salvation by our God.
Sing joyfully to the LORD, all you lands;
  break into song; sing praise.

℟. All the ends of the earth have seen the saving power of God.

Sing praise to the LORD with the harp,
with the harp and melodious song.
With trumpets and the sound of the horn
sing joyfully before the King, the LORD.

℟. All the ends of the earth have seen the saving power of God.

See Appendix, p. 201, for Second Reading

Reflecting on Living the Gospel

The Baptist comes as a voice for a time; Jesus is the Word for all eternity. The Word is the radiance of the Father's glory; the Baptist is the lamp-carrier who becomes unnecessary when the Light is among us. And John the Baptist is humbly content to be only voice and lamp. Such humble witness to the Word, and not to ourselves, is the privilege of all who accept the Word into their lives. It's not an optional extra for those who have heard the Word and seen the Light.

Connecting the Responsorial Psalm to the Readings

Today's gospel contains our great hope as Christians. We recognize that the life of Jesus is "the light of the human race." It is a "light [that] shines in the darkness, / and the darkness has not overcome it." In our world today there continues to be great darkness, and yet we know that the light is stronger. Our responsorial psalm proclaims, "All the ends of the earth have seen the saving power of God." Just as a single match can light up the darkest cave, the love of God dispels hatred, the life of God defeats death, and the light of God illuminates all areas of the earth where hope, faith, and charity persist.

Psalmist Preparation

As children of the light, how are we called to enlighten the darkness within ourselves, our families, and our communities so that God's saving power might be revealed to all?

Prayer

Redeeming God,
Today is born our savior, Christ the Lord!
Make us fully aware of the magnificent in-breaking
into our time and space that your incarnation was and continues to be.
Indeed, *all the ends of the earth have seen the saving power of God.*
We are humbled, we are grateful. Amen.

THE HOLY FAMILY OF JESUS, MARY, AND JOSEPH

DECEMBER 27, 2020

Gospel (Luke 2:22-40 [or 2:22, 39-40]; L17B)

When the days were completed for their purification according to the law of Moses, they took him up to Jerusalem to present him to the Lord, just as it is written in the law of the Lord, *Every male that opens the womb shall be consecrated to the Lord,* and to offer the sacrifice of *a pair of turtledoves or two young pigeons,* in accordance with the dictate in the law of the Lord.

Now there was a man in Jerusalem whose name was Simeon. This man was righteous and devout, awaiting the consolation of Israel, and the Holy Spirit was upon him. It had been revealed to him by the Holy Spirit that he should not see death before he had seen the Christ of the Lord. He came in the Spirit into the temple; and when the parents brought in the child Jesus to perform the custom of the law in regard to him, he took him into his arms and blessed God, saying:

"Now, Master, you may let your servant go
in peace, according to your word,
for my eyes have seen your salvation,
which you prepared in sight of all the peoples,
a light for revelation to the Gentiles,
and glory for your people Israel."

The child's father and mother were amazed at what was said about him; and Simeon blessed them and said to Mary his mother, "Behold, this child is destined for the fall and rise of many in Israel, and to be a sign that will be contradicted—and you yourself a sword will pierce—so that the thoughts of many hearts may be revealed." There was also a prophetess, Anna, the daughter of Phanuel, of the tribe of Asher. She was advanced in years, having lived seven years with her husband after her marriage, and then as a widow until she was eighty-four. She never left the temple, but worshiped night and day with fasting and prayer. And coming forward at that very time, she gave thanks to God and spoke about the child to all who were awaiting the redemption of Jerusalem.

When they had fulfilled all the prescriptions of the law of the Lord, they returned to Galilee, to their own town of Nazareth. The child grew and became strong, filled with wisdom; and the favor of God was upon him.

First Reading **(Sir 3:2-6, 12-14 [or Gen 15:1-6; 21:1-3])**

God sets a father in honor over his children;
  a mother's authority he confirms over her sons.
Whoever honors his father atones for sins,
  and preserves himself from them.
When he prays, he is heard;
  he stores up riches who reveres his mother.
Whoever honors his father is gladdened by children,
  and, when he prays, is heard.
Whoever reveres his father will live a long life;
  he who obeys his father brings comfort to his mother.

My son, take care of your father when he is old;
  grieve him not as long as he lives.
Even if his mind fail, be considerate of him;
  revile him not all the days of his life;
kindness to a father will not be forgotten,
  firmly planted against the debt of your sins
  —a house raised in justice to you.

Responsorial Psalm **(Ps 128:1-2, 3, 4-5 [or Ps 105:1-2, 3-4, 6-7, 8-9])**

℟. (cf. 1) Blessed are those who fear the Lord and walk in his ways.

Blessed is everyone who fears the LORD,
  who walks in his ways!
For you shall eat the fruit of your handiwork;
  blessed shall you be, and favored.

℟. Blessed are those who fear the Lord and walk in his ways.

Your wife shall be like a fruitful vine
  in the recesses of your home;
your children like olive plants
  around your table.

℟. Blessed are those who fear the Lord and walk in his ways.

Behold, thus is the man blessed
who fears the LORD.
The LORD bless you from Zion:
may you see the prosperity of Jerusalem
all the days of your life.

℟. Blessed are those who fear the Lord and walk in his ways.

See Appendix, p. 201, for Second Reading

Reflecting on Living the Gospel

Every family, whether gifted with many children or none or one, has a role to play in God's dramatic story of salvation and shares in the miraculous gift of hope children represent. Each child has been willed by God to serve a unique purpose. Mary and Joseph were "amazed at what was said about" Jesus, for he was the fulfillment of all hopes. But in the reality of the Holy Family, we see the miraculous nature of every child and every family reflected.

Connecting the Responsorial Psalm to the Readings

Forty days after the birth of Jesus, Mary and Joseph leave Bethlehem to begin the trek back home to Nazareth. On the way, they stop at the temple in Jerusalem to fulfill "the dictate in the law of the Lord." In Luke's gospel, this is the first journey that Mary and Joseph undertake with their newborn son. Today's psalm response also calls to mind a journey. We are told, "Blessed are those who fear the Lord and walk in his ways." Just as traveling with a newborn requires parents to be attentive to the rhythms and needs of their child, entering into the journey of faith calls us to be attentive to the actions and voice of God prompting us forward or holding us back.

Psalmist Preparation

In the spiritual life, how do you seek to walk in the "ways" of God?

THE HOLY FAMILY OF JESUS, MARY, AND JOSEPH

Prayer

Father, Son, and Spirit,
in your very being you are a community of love.
In our families, grant us patience, persistence, and forgiveness,
that we too may be communities of love.
Be mindful of your promise to be with us always,
for you are *the Lord* who *remembers his covenant forever.* Amen.

SOLEMNITY OF MARY, THE HOLY MOTHER OF GOD

JANUARY 1, 2021

***Gospel* (Luke 2:16-21; L18ABC)**

The shepherds went in haste to Bethlehem and found Mary and Joseph, and the infant lying in the manger. When they saw this, they made known the message that had been told them about this child. All who heard it were amazed by what had been told them by the shepherds. And Mary kept all these things, reflecting on them in her heart. Then the shepherds returned, glorifying and praising God for all they had heard and seen, just as it had been told to them.

When eight days were completed for his circumcision, he was named Jesus, the name given him by the angel before he was conceived in the womb.

***First Reading* (Num 6:22-27)**

The LORD said to Moses: "Speak to Aaron and his sons and tell them: This is how you shall bless the Israelites. Say to them:

The LORD bless you and keep you!
The LORD let his face shine upon you, and be gracious to you!
The LORD look upon you kindly and give you peace!

So shall they invoke my name upon the Israelites, and I will bless them."

***Responsorial Psalm* (Ps 67:2-3, 5, 6, 8)**

℟. (2a) May God bless us in his mercy.

May God have pity on us and bless us;
may he let his face shine upon us.
So may your way be known upon earth;
among all nations, your salvation.

℟. May God bless us in his mercy.

May the nations be glad and exult
because you rule the peoples in equity;
the nations on the earth you guide.

℟. May God bless us in his mercy.

May the peoples praise you, O God;
 may all the peoples praise you!
May God bless us,
 and may all the ends of the earth fear him!

℟. May God bless us in his mercy.

See Appendix, p. 202, for Second Reading

Reflecting on Living the Gospel

As we gaze on this peaceful woman, we can appreciate how appropriate it is that January 1 has been chosen by the church as the day on which we pray for world peace. Like her, we are called to gaze on the child who is the Prince of Peace. It is his reign, not the Pax Romana, not the Pax Americana, nor any other political maneuvering, that will make God's way known upon earth. The responsibility for peace is now in our hands.

Connecting the Responsorial Psalm to the Readings

Today we begin a new calendar year by asking God for his blessing and his mercy. In the first reading the Lord instructs Moses on how Aaron is to bless the people: "The Lord bless you and keep you! / The Lord let his face shine upon you, and be gracious to you! / The Lord look upon you kindly and give you peace!" Though Aaron is the one who is to speak these words, God assures Moses that through this invocation God himself "will bless them."

Psalmist Preparation

As we begin this new year of ministry and service let us ponder the ways God has blessed us in the past and look with hope toward the future and the blessings that are awaiting us in the days, weeks, and months to come.

Prayer

God of justice and peace,
you too are a God of mercy where so often it is undeserved.
Help us today to be instruments of your peace,
and, like Mary, bring your holy presence to birth wherever we go.
As this new year begins, *may God bless us in his mercy.* Amen.

JANUARY 3, 2021

Gospel **(Matt 2:1-12; L20ABC)**

When Jesus was born in Bethlehem of Judea, in the days of King Herod, behold, magi from the east arrived in Jerusalem, saying, "Where is the newborn king of the Jews? We saw his star at its rising and have come to do him homage." When King Herod heard this, he was greatly troubled, and all Jerusalem with him. Assembling all the chief priests and the scribes of the people, he inquired of them where the Christ was to be born. They said to him, "In Bethlehem of Judea, for thus it has been written through the prophet:

And you, Bethlehem, land of Judah,
are by no means least among the rulers of Judah;
since from you shall come a ruler,
who is to shepherd my people Israel."

Then Herod called the magi secretly and ascertained from them the time of the star's appearance. He sent them to Bethlehem and said, "Go and search diligently for the child. When you have found him, bring me word, that I too may go and do him homage." After their audience with the king they set out. And behold, the star that they had seen at its rising preceded them, until it came and stopped over the place where the child was. They were overjoyed at seeing the star, and on entering the house they saw the child with Mary his mother. They prostrated themselves and did him homage. Then they opened their treasures and offered him gifts of gold, frankincense, and myrrh. And having been warned in a dream not to return to Herod, they departed for their country by another way.

First Reading **(Isa 60:1-6)**

Rise up in splendor, Jerusalem! Your light has come,
the glory of the Lord shines upon you.
See, darkness covers the earth,
and thick clouds cover the peoples;
but upon you the LORD shines,
and over you appears his glory.

Nations shall walk by your light,
  and kings by your shining radiance.
Raise your eyes and look about;
  they all gather and come to you:
your sons come from afar,
  and your daughters in the arms of their nurses.

Then you shall be radiant at what you see,
  your heart shall throb and overflow,
for the riches of the sea shall be emptied out before you,
  the wealth of nations shall be brought to you.
Caravans of camels shall fill you,
  dromedaries from Midian and Ephah;
all from Sheba shall come
  bearing gold and frankincense,
  and proclaiming the praises of the LORD.

***Responsorial Psalm* (Ps 72:1-2, 7-8, 10-11, 12-13)**

℟. (cf. 11) Lord, every nation on earth will adore you.

O God, with your judgment endow the king,
  and with your justice, the king's son;
he shall govern your people with justice
  and your afflicted ones with judgment.

℟. Lord, every nation on earth will adore you.

Justice shall flower in his days,
  and profound peace, till the moon be no more.
May he rule from sea to sea,
  and from the River to the ends of the earth.

℟. Lord, every nation on earth will adore you.

The kings of Tarshish and the Isles shall offer gifts;
  the kings of Arabia and Seba shall bring tribute.
All kings shall pay him homage,
  all nations shall serve him.

℟. Lord, every nation on earth will adore you.

For he shall rescue the poor when he cries out,
  and the afflicted when he has no one to help him.
He shall have pity for the lowly and the poor;
  the lives of the poor he shall save.

℟. Lord, every nation on earth will adore you.

See Appendix, p. 202, for Second Reading

Reflecting on Living the Gospel

When we place the magi in our Christmas crib, the truth that their visit declares and the symbolism that their presence in the crib proclaims is the gospel truth that Jesus is king for all the nations of the earth. This is what we pray for in the words of the responsorial Psalm 72: the establishment of God's kingdom of justice and peace throughout the world so that the rights of the poor and helpless are respected and the cries of the needy are answered.

Connecting the Responsorial Psalm to the Readings

Today's psalm gives us more images for what the fullness of God's kingdom will look like when "every nation on earth will adore" the Creator. We are told that this will be a time of justice and "profound peace, till the moon be no more." This time is also set apart by care for the poor whose lives God "shall save."

Psalmist Preparation

With its images of peace and justice, today's psalm is one of comfort, hope, and also of challenge. When we look at the world, we can see many places where this peace and justice do not yet reign, areas where the lives of the poor are endangered and threatened. As you prepare to lead the people of God in prayer, consider how you are attending to the work of peace and justice and care for the poor in your own life.

Prayer

Ever-giving God,
while we offer you today the meager gifts we have,
help us to be mindful of the gifts you always bestow on us all:
faith, love, joy, mercy, forgiveness: the list never ends.
Truly, *Lord, every nation on earth will adore you*
in praise of your generosity. Amen.

***Gospel* (Mark 1:7-11; L21B)**

This is what John the Baptist proclaimed: "One mightier than I is coming after me. I am not worthy to stoop and loosen the thongs of his sandals. I have baptized you with water; he will baptize you with the Holy Spirit."

It happened in those days that Jesus came from Nazareth of Galilee and was baptized in the Jordan by John. On coming up out of the water he saw the heavens being torn open and the Spirit, like a dove, descending upon him. And a voice came from the heavens, "You are my beloved Son; with you I am well pleased."

***First Reading* (Isa 42:1-4, 6-7 [or Isa 55:1-11])**

Thus says the LORD:
Here is my servant whom I uphold,
  my chosen one with whom I am pleased,
upon whom I have put my spirit;
  he shall bring forth justice to the nations,
not crying out, not shouting,
  not making his voice heard in the street.
A bruised reed he shall not break,
  and a smoldering wick he shall not quench,
until he establishes justice on the earth;
  the coastlands will wait for his teaching.

I, the LORD, have called you for the victory of justice,
  I have grasped you by the hand;
I formed you, and set you
  as a covenant of the people,
  a light for the nations,
to open the eyes of the blind,
  to bring out prisoners from confinement,
  and from the dungeon, those who live in darkness.

***Responsorial Psalm* (Ps 29:1-2, 3-4, 3, 9-10 [or Isa 12:2-3, 4bcd, 5-6])**

℟. (11b) The Lord will bless his people with peace.

Give to the LORD, you sons of God,
 give to the LORD glory and praise,
give to the LORD the glory due his name;
 adore the LORD in holy attire.

℟. The Lord will bless his people with peace.

The voice of the LORD is over the waters,
 the LORD, over vast waters.
The voice of the LORD is mighty;
 the voice of the LORD is majestic.

℟. The Lord will bless his people with peace.

The God of glory thunders,
 and in his temple all say, "Glory!"
The LORD is enthroned above the flood;
 the LORD is enthroned as king forever.

℟. The Lord will bless his people with peace.

See Appendix, p. 202, for Second Reading

Reflecting on Living the Gospel

This gospel is a declaration of who Jesus is to Mark's church, a statement of their self-understanding as disciples of the new messianic times who are sons and daughters of the Father because they are baptized into the Spirit-filled and Beloved Son, and commissioned to serve in his name. Throughout Mark's gospel, those who follow Jesus will struggle to understand what is revealed to Jesus as he rises from the waters: that humanity, despite its sinfulness, is loved with the prodigal love of God.

Connecting the Responsorial Psalm to the Readings

When Jesus comes out of the waters, he witnesses "the Spirit, like a dove, descending upon him." In the dove we find a symbol of peace, hearkening back to the dove who brought Noah an olive branch to signal the end of the great flood and a new covenant between God and humans. In this covenant, God promised to never again "strike down every living being, as I have done" (Genesis 8:21; NABRE). At the beginning of his public ministry, Jesus receives an affirmation of his identity as God's beloved Son who is anointed to bring God's spirit of peace and love to all people. Today's psalm once again proclaims God's deep desire to "bless his people with peace."

Psalmist Preparation

Where in your life are you in need of the peace of God, which casts out all anxieties, doubts, and fears?

Prayer

God, mighty and vast,
you use simple and ubiquitous water
to reveal saving grace and cleanse us from sin.
As on a calm day a sea becomes like glass,
so too your son *will bless his people with peace,*
he who lives and reigns forever and ever. Amen.

JANUARY 17, 2021

***Gospel* (John 1:35-42; L65B)**

John was standing with two of his disciples, and as he watched Jesus walk by, he said, "Behold, the Lamb of God." The two disciples heard what he said and followed Jesus. Jesus turned and saw them following him and said to them, "What are you looking for?" They said to him, "Rabbi"—which translated means Teacher—, "where are you staying?" He said to them, "Come, and you will see." So they went and saw where Jesus was staying, and they stayed with him that day. It was about four in the afternoon. Andrew, the brother of Simon Peter, was one of the two who heard John and followed Jesus. He first found his own brother Simon and told him, "We have found the Messiah"—which is translated Christ. Then he brought him to Jesus. Jesus looked at him and said, "You are Simon the son of John; you will be called Cephas"—which is translated Peter.

***First Reading* (1 Sam 3:3b-10, 19)**

Samuel was sleeping in the temple of the LORD where the ark of God was. The LORD called to Samuel, who answered, "Here I am." Samuel ran to Eli and said, "Here I am. You called me." "I did not call you," Eli said. "Go back to sleep." So he went back to sleep. Again the LORD called Samuel, who rose and went to Eli. "Here I am," he said. "You called me." But Eli answered, "I did not call you, my son. Go back to sleep."

At that time Samuel was not familiar with the LORD, because the LORD had not revealed anything to him as yet. The LORD called Samuel again, for the third time. Getting up and going to Eli, he said, "Here I am. You called me." Then Eli understood that the LORD was calling the youth. So he said to Samuel, "Go to sleep, and if you are called, reply, 'Speak, LORD, for your servant is listening.'" When Samuel went to sleep in his place, the LORD came and revealed his presence, calling out as before, "Samuel, Samuel!" Samuel answered, "Speak, for your servant is listening."

Samuel grew up, and the LORD was with him, not permitting any word of his to be without effect.

Responsorial Psalm **(Ps 40:2, 4, 7-8, 8-9, 10)**

℟. (8a and 9a) Here am I, Lord; I come to do your will.

I have waited, waited for the LORD,
  and he stooped toward me and heard my cry.
And he put a new song into my mouth,
  a hymn to our God.

℟. Here am I, Lord; I come to do your will.

Sacrifice or offering you wished not,
  but ears open to obedience you gave me.
Holocausts or sin-offerings you sought not;
  then said I, "Behold I come."

℟. Here am I, Lord; I come to do your will.

"In the written scroll it is prescribed for me,
to do your will, O my God, is my delight,
  and your law is within my heart!"

℟. Here am I, Lord; I come to do your will.

I announced your justice in the vast assembly;
  I did not restrain my lips, as you, O LORD, know.

℟. Here am I, Lord; I come to do your will.

Second Reading **(1 Cor 6:13c-15a, 17-20)**

Reflecting on Living the Gospel

This gospel proclaims that all discipleship is an active and involving relationship with Jesus: a following, seeking, staying, finding, and dialoguing with him. We hear how each decision to follow Jesus is a response to a statement about Jesus's identity as Lamb of God, Rabbi, Messiah, by people whose ears and hearts are open to the Word of God, who hear his invitation through the words of friend or stranger, through events of joy or sorrow, or who discern a moment of religious significance in the everyday.

Connecting the Responsorial Psalm to the Readings

In today's readings we are given two similar prayers with which to ponder the life of discipleship. The psalm refrain "Here am I, Lord; I come to do your will" is very similar to Samuel's response to the divine voice calling him by name: "Speak, LORD, for your servant is listening." Both express an awareness of God's presence and also complete trust in God's plan and action in their lives. As the psalmist recounts, however, the life of discipleship is not always straightforward and can require a good deal of patience ("I have waited, waited for the Lord").

Psalmist Preparation

This week, take time to pray with the words from the psalm response. What does it mean to show up each day in your relationship with God and to be eager to do God's will?

Prayer

Good and gracious God,
you only desire the best for us, giving us what we need in due season.
Grant us the sureness to trust in you, that we might always be willing to pray:
Here am I, Lord; I come to do your will.
Through Christ our Lord. Amen.

***Gospel* (Mark 1:14-20; L68B)**

After John had been arrested, Jesus came to Galilee proclaiming the gospel of God: "This is the time of fulfillment. The kingdom of God is at hand. Repent, and believe in the gospel."

As he passed by the Sea of Galilee, he saw Simon and his brother Andrew casting their nets into the sea; they were fishermen. Jesus said to them, "Come after me, and I will make you fishers of men." Then they abandoned their nets and followed him. He walked along a little farther and saw James, the son of Zebedee, and his brother John. They too were in a boat mending their nets. Then he called them. So they left their father Zebedee in the boat along with the hired men and followed him.

***First Reading* (Jonah 3:1-5, 10)**

The word of the LORD came to Jonah, saying: "Set out for the great city of Nineveh, and announce to it the message that I will tell you." So Jonah made ready and went to Nineveh, according to the LORD's bidding. Now Nineveh was an enormously large city; it took three days to go through it. Jonah began his journey through the city, and had gone but a single day's walk announcing, "Forty days more and Nineveh shall be destroyed," when the people of Nineveh believed God; they proclaimed a fast and all of them, great and small, put on sackcloth.

When God saw by their actions how they turned from their evil way, he repented of the evil that he had threatened to do to them; he did not carry it out.

***Responsorial Psalm* (Ps 25:4-5, 6-7, 8-9)**

℟. (4a) Teach me your ways, O Lord.

Your ways, O LORD, make known to me;
teach me your paths,
Guide me in your truth and teach me,
for you are God my savior.

℟. Teach me your ways, O Lord.

Remember that your compassion, O LORD,
and your love are from of old.
In your kindness remember me,
because of your goodness, O LORD.

℟. Teach me your ways, O Lord.

Good and upright is the LORD;
thus he shows sinners the way.
He guides the humble to justice
and teaches the humble his way.

℟. Teach me your ways, O Lord.

***Second Reading* (1 Cor 7:29-31)**

Reflecting on Living the Gospel

Jesus does not issue orders to his followers like a charismatic military leader; he offers no rallying call to a revolutionary war, but he does make promises. Do we live as though we believe these promises? How constant, how radical are we in our following of Jesus to which we are invited by our baptism? How discerning of its demands are we in our contemporary society, and has Jesus priority in our lives?

Connecting the Responsorial Psalm to the Readings

God's loving compassion is affirmed by the psalmist who proclaims, "Good and upright is the Lord; / thus he shows sinners the way." This truth can be comforting when we apply it to ourselves and our own sinfulness, but challenging when we consider this boundless compassion enveloping those who have hurt us. Though the first reading offers only a portion of the book of Jonah, we know how this story ends. The Ninevites, who had crushed the northern kingdom of Israel and then ravaged Jerusalem in 701 BC, repent of their evil ways and are forgiven by God. Although this tale is fiction, it would have been difficult for the Israelites to swallow. We could place ourselves in this tale by thinking of the Ninevites as a nation or ideological group that has waged war or acts of terror on our own nation or members of our religion.

Psalmist Preparation

Our responsorial psalm asks, "Teach me your ways, O Lord." One of these ways is God's unconditional love and forgiveness. How can you live deeper into this attribute of God this week?

Prayer

God of kindness,
you ask us to strive for holiness.
Your words are spirit and life;
may we always learn your disciplines and grow closer to you day by day.
Teach me your ways, O Lord, teach us all your ways. Save us. Amen.

JANUARY 31, 2021

***Gospel* (Mark 1:21-28; L71B)**

Then they came to Capernaum, and on the sabbath Jesus entered the synagogue and taught. The people were astonished at his teaching, for he taught them as one having authority and not as the scribes. In their synagogue was a man with an unclean spirit; he cried out, "What have you to do with us, Jesus of Nazareth? Have you come to destroy us? I know who you are—the Holy One of God!" Jesus rebuked him and said, "Quiet! Come out of him!" The unclean spirit convulsed him and with a loud cry came out of him. All were amazed and asked one another, "What is this? A new teaching with authority. He commands even the unclean spirits and they obey him." His fame spread everywhere throughout the whole region of Galilee.

***First Reading* (Deut 18:15-20)**

Moses spoke to all the people, saying: "A prophet like me will the LORD, your God, raise up for you from among your own kin; to him you shall listen. This is exactly what you requested of the LORD, your God, at Horeb on the day of the assembly, when you said, 'Let us not again hear the voice of the LORD, our God, nor see this great fire any more, lest we die.' And the LORD said to me, 'This was well said. I will raise up for them a prophet like you from among their kin, and will put my words into his mouth; he shall tell them all that I command him. Whoever will not listen to my words which he speaks in my name, I myself will make him answer for it. But if a prophet presumes to speak in my name an oracle that I have not commanded him to speak, or speaks in the name of other gods, he shall die.'"

***Responsorial Psalm* (Ps 95:1-2, 6-7, 7-9)**

℟. (8) If today you hear his voice, harden not your hearts.

Come, let us sing joyfully to the LORD;
  let us acclaim the rock of our salvation.
Let us come into his presence with thanksgiving;
  let us joyfully sing psalms to him.

℟. If today you hear his voice, harden not your hearts.

Come, let us bow down in worship;
  let us kneel before the LORD who made us.
For he is our God,
  and we are the people he shepherds, the flock he guides.

℟. If today you hear his voice, harden not your hearts.

Oh, that today you would hear his voice:
  "Harden not your hearts as at Meribah,
  as in the day of Massah in the desert,
Where your fathers tempted me;
  they tested me though they had seen my works."

℟. If today you hear his voice, harden not your hearts.

Second Reading (1 Cor 7:32-35)

Reflecting on Living the Gospel

Jesus healed the man of the unclean spirit, and the people called this action of Jesus a "teaching": "[They] asked one another, 'What is this? A new teaching with authority.'" It is God's presence and power that is the lesson not only to learn but to encounter. Ultimately we are all students of the one teacher, whose authority is ordered to our salvation and joy. From this school we never graduate; this teacher is always guiding us. This education is perfected for our final purpose: to know God.

Connecting the Responsorial Psalm to the Readings

Today's psalm calls to mind another event from the exodus: when the Israelites, freed from slavery in Egypt but before meeting God at Mount Sinai, grumble to Moses due to their thirst. They even go so far as to ask him, "Why then did you bring us up out of Egypt? To have us die of thirst with our children and our livestock?" (Exod 17:3; NABRE). Although the people had seen the power of the Lord at work in their escape from Egypt, they do not yet believe that God will continue to provide for all of their needs. In doubt and bitterness they quarrel and test the Lord, asking, "Is the Lord in our midst or not?" (Exod 17:7; NABRE).

Psalmist Preparation

The psalmist invites us, even as we encounter our own trials and temptations, to "harden not your hearts." How is God calling you to trust in his goodness?

Prayer

Creator,
your breath which voiced all things into being still moves today.
A gentle whisper is difficult to notice in the hectic pace of our lives.
Grant us stillness and an attentiveness to your son,
so that, *if today* we *hear his voice,*
our stony hearts will be open to his word. Amen.

***Gospel* (Mark 1:29-39; L74B)**

On leaving the synagogue Jesus entered the house of Simon and Andrew with James and John. Simon's mother-in-law lay sick with a fever. They immediately told him about her. He approached, grasped her hand, and helped her up. Then the fever left her and she waited on them.

When it was evening, after sunset, they brought to him all who were ill or possessed by demons. The whole town was gathered at the door. He cured many who were sick with various diseases, and he drove out many demons, not permitting them to speak because they knew him.

Rising very early before dawn, he left and went off to a deserted place, where he prayed. Simon and those who were with him pursued him and on finding him said, "Everyone is looking for you." He told them, "Let us go on to the nearby villages that I may preach there also. For this purpose have I come." So he went into their synagogues, preaching and driving out demons throughout the whole of Galilee.

***First Reading* (Job 7:1-4, 6-7)**

Job spoke, saying:

Is not man's life on earth a drudgery?
  Are not his days those of hirelings?
He is a slave who longs for the shade,
  a hireling who waits for his wages.
So I have been assigned months of misery,
  and troubled nights have been allotted to me.
If in bed I say, "When shall I arise?"
  then the night drags on;
  I am filled with restlessness until the dawn.
My days are swifter than a weaver's shuttle;
  they come to an end without hope.
Remember that my life is like the wind;
  I shall not see happiness again.

Responsorial Psalm (Ps 147:1-2, 3-4, 5-6)

℟. (cf. 3a) Praise the Lord, who heals the brokenhearted.
or: ℟. Alleluia.

Praise the LORD, for he is good;
  sing praise to our God, for he is gracious;
  it is fitting to praise him.
The LORD rebuilds Jerusalem;
  the dispersed of Israel he gathers.

℟. Praise the Lord, who heals the brokenhearted. *or:* ℟. Alleluia.

He heals the brokenhearted
  and binds up their wounds.
He tells the number of the stars;
  he calls each by name.

℟. Praise the Lord, who heals the brokenhearted. *or:* ℟. Alleluia.

Great is our Lord and mighty in power;
  to his wisdom there is no limit.
The LORD sustains the lowly;
  the wicked he casts to the ground.

℟. Praise the Lord, who heals the brokenhearted. *or:* ℟. Alleluia.

Second Reading (1 Cor 9:16-19, 22-23)

Reflecting on Living the Gospel

In the healing of Simon's mother-in-law we have a vignette of the mission of Jesus, the free man, who cares nothing for taboos that prohibited the touching of a woman not one's wife, and especially on the Sabbath. Jesus has healed the tormented man in the synagogue, and he will make no discrimination between male and female, even though to hold the hand of the sick woman could earn him the accusation of ritual uncleanness. Compassion has a more urgent hold on Jesus.

Connecting the Responsorial Psalm to the Readings

Today's psalm references God's mighty acts of mercy and compassion in returning the people of Israel to their land after the Babylonian exile. After seeing their country ravaged and the temple destroyed, it would not be an overstatement to say the people's hearts had been collectively broken as they were taken away into exile as the spoils of conquest. Much like the story of Job, it seems like this is the worst that a country or an individual could face. And yet, the psalmist stresses that the people are not alone. Though the temple—the particular place of encounter with God—is no more, their God accompanies them into exile, tends to their broken hearts, and finally leads them home again.

Psalmist Preparation

How have you experienced God as a healer to the brokenhearted?

Prayer

God of restoration,
you bring wholeness to the broken,
and a peace only you can give to the conflicted.
May we know your healing in profound and unexpected ways,
and rise to praise your name, you *who heals the brokenhearted.*
We make this prayer through your son, healer and redeemer. Amen.

FEBRUARY 14, 2021

***Gospel* (Mark 1:40-45; L77B)**

A leper came to Jesus and kneeling down begged him and said, "If you wish, you can make me clean." Moved with pity, he stretched out his hand, touched him, and said to him, "I do will it. Be made clean." The leprosy left him immediately, and he was made clean. Then, warning him sternly, he dismissed him at once.

He said to him, "See that you tell no one anything, but go, show yourself to the priest and offer for your cleansing what Moses prescribed; that will be proof for them."

The man went away and began to publicize the whole matter. He spread the report abroad so that it was impossible for Jesus to enter a town openly. He remained outside in deserted places, and people kept coming to him from everywhere.

***First Reading* (Lev 13:1-2, 44-46)**

The LORD said to Moses and Aaron, "If someone has on his skin a scab or pustule or blotch which appears to be the sore of leprosy, he shall be brought to Aaron, the priest, or to one of the priests among his descendants. If the man is leprous and unclean, the priest shall declare him unclean by reason of the sore on his head.

"The one who bears the sore of leprosy shall keep his garments rent and his head bare, and shall muffle his beard; he shall cry out, 'Unclean, unclean!' As long as the sore is on him he shall declare himself unclean, since he is in fact unclean. He shall dwell apart, making his abode outside the camp."

Responsorial Psalm **(Ps 32:1-2, 5, 11)**

℟. (7) I turn to you, Lord, in time of trouble, and you fill me with the joy of salvation.

Blessed is he whose fault is taken away,
whose sin is covered.
Blessed the man to whom the LORD imputes not guilt,
in whose spirit there is no guile.

℟. I turn to you, Lord, in time of trouble, and you fill me with the joy of salvation.

Then I acknowledged my sin to you,
my guilt I covered not.
I said, "I confess my faults to the LORD,"
and you took away the guilt of my sin.

℟. I turn to you, Lord, in time of trouble, and you fill me with the joy of salvation.

Be glad in the LORD and rejoice, you just;
exult, all you upright of heart.

℟. I turn to you, Lord, in time of trouble, and you fill me with the joy of salvation.

Second Reading **(1 Cor 10:31–11:1)**

Reflecting on Living the Gospel
In the gospel, Jesus is approached by a leper. He is moved by compassion, the deep gut-wrenching response that identifies with the suffering of another. Who are today's "lepers," people whom some consider as "polluting" society by their differences in race, culture, social mores, or physical and intellectual disabilities? What are our attitudes to those we might consider as weakening the moral fiber of society—the drug addicts, the HIV/AIDS sufferers, those in prison? Are we on the side of harsh, punitive justice or compassionate restorative justice?

Connecting the Responsorial Psalm to the Readings
The leper approaches Jesus and tells him, "If you wish, you can make me clean." In these simple words the man names both who he is and who he believes Jesus to be. He acknowledges his own affliction while also asserting Jesus's power to cleanse and to heal. Today's psalm offers us much the

same framework for reconciliation, first in revealing oneself truthfully to God ("I acknowledged my sin to you / my guilt I covered not") and then lifting up God's power to restore ("you took away the guilt of my sin").

Psalmist Preparation

The season of Lent will soon be upon us; what sin or weakness is God calling you to bring before him so that he might take it away and bring healing?

Prayer

Divine Consoler,
in time of trouble, we have always and will always *turn to you.*
There is no one else who can offer your solace and comfort,
no one else who brings complete healing and peace.
Fill us *with the joy of salvation.*
Through Christ our Lord. Amen.

***Gospel* (Matt 6:1-6, 16-18; L219)**

Jesus said to his disciples: "Take care not to perform righteous deeds in order that people may see them; otherwise, you will have no recompense from your heavenly Father. When you give alms, do not blow a trumpet before you, as the hypocrites do in the synagogues and in the streets to win the praise of others. Amen, I say to you, they have received their reward. But when you give alms, do not let your left hand know what your right is doing, so that your almsgiving may be secret. And your Father who sees in secret will repay you.

"When you pray, do not be like the hypocrites, who love to stand and pray in the synagogues and on street corners so that others may see them. Amen, I say to you, they have received their reward. But when you pray, go to your inner room, close the door, and pray to your Father in secret. And your Father who sees in secret will repay you.

"When you fast, do not look gloomy like the hypocrites. They neglect their appearance, so that they may appear to others to be fasting. Amen, I say to you, they have received their reward. But when you fast, anoint your head and wash your face, so that you may not appear to be fasting, except to your Father who is hidden. And your Father who sees what is hidden will repay you."

***First Reading* (Joel 2:12-18)**

Even now, says the LORD,
  return to me with your whole heart,
  with fasting, and weeping, and mourning;
Rend your hearts, not your garments,
  and return to the LORD, your God.
For gracious and merciful is he,
  slow to anger, rich in kindness,
  and relenting in punishment.
Perhaps he will again relent
  and leave behind him a blessing,

Offerings and libations
  for the LORD, your God.
Blow the trumpet in Zion!
  proclaim a fast,
  call an assembly;
Gather the people,
  notify the congregation;
Assemble the elders,
  gather the children
  and the infants at the breast;
Let the bridegroom quit his room,
  and the bride her chamber.
Between the porch and the altar
  let the priests, the ministers of the LORD, weep,
And say, "Spare, O LORD, your people,
  and make not your heritage a reproach,
  with the nations ruling over them!
Why should they say among the peoples,
  'Where is their God?'"

Then the LORD was stirred to concern for his land
  and took pity on his people.

***Responsorial Psalm* (Ps 51:3-4, 5-6ab, 12-13, 14 and 17)**

℟. (see 3a) Be merciful, O Lord, for we have sinned.

Have mercy on me, O God, in your goodness;
  in the greatness of your compassion wipe out my offense.
Thoroughly wash me from my guilt
  and of my sin cleanse me.

℟. Be merciful, O Lord, for we have sinned.

For I acknowledge my offense,
  and my sin is before me always:
"Against you only have I sinned,
  and done what is evil in your sight."

℟. Be merciful, O Lord, for we have sinned.

A clean heart create for me, O God,
  and a steadfast spirit renew within me.
Cast me not out from your presence,
  and your Holy Spirit take not from me.

℟. Be merciful, O Lord, for we have sinned.

Give me back the joy of your salvation,
  and a willing spirit sustain in me.
O Lord, open my lips,
  and my mouth shall proclaim your praise.

℟. Be merciful, O Lord, for we have sinned.

See Appendix, p. 202, for Second Reading

Reflecting on Living the Gospel

Ash Wednesday calls us into the Lenten weeks of keeping warm the embers of our Christian discipleship through a renewed commitment to prayer, to fasting, and to almsgiving, so that the breath of the Easter Jesus may rekindle in us the fire of our baptism. The Sundays of Lent retain their character as commemorations of the resurrection of the Lord, and so the reminder that Lent is a preparation for the celebration of Easter is woven like a golden thread through the season's darker days.

Connecting the Responsorial Psalm to the Readings

Each Ash Wednesday we gather to pray together, "Be merciful, O Lord, for we have sinned." On either side of this psalm where we admit guilt, offense, and evil, we are assured by both the prophet Joel and the apostle Paul that no matter what action or inaction has brought us to repentance, our God stands ready to save. Through the prophet God calls to his wayward people, "Even now . . . return to me with your whole heart" and Paul assures us that no matter what has come before it, today "is the day of salvation."

Psalmist Preparation

True repentance requires us to acknowledge our guilt and to feel sorrow for the offense that we have caused to God and others. This Lent, with acts of prayer, almsgiving, and fasting, how will you live out your own repentance and also your faith in the infinite mercy of God?

Prayer

Forgiving God,
you never tire of waiting for repentant hearts to return to you.
You never mark iniquities; you offer bountiful love.
Be merciful, O Lord, for we have sinned.
Show us your face, and we shall be saved. Amen.

Gospel **(Mark 1:12-15; L23B)**

The Spirit drove Jesus out into the desert, and he remained in the desert for forty days, tempted by Satan. He was among wild beasts, and the angels ministered to him.

After John had been arrested, Jesus came to Galilee proclaiming the gospel of God: "This is the time of fulfillment. The kingdom of God is at hand. Repent, and believe in the gospel."

First Reading **(Gen 9:8-15)**

God said to Noah and to his sons with him: "See, I am now establishing my covenant with you and your descendants after you and with every living creature that was with you: all the birds, and the various tame and wild animals that were with you and came out of the ark. I will establish my covenant with you, that never again shall all bodily creatures be destroyed by the waters of a flood; there shall not be another flood to devastate the earth." God added: "This is the sign that I am giving for all ages to come, of the covenant between me and you and every living creature with you: I set my bow in the clouds to serve as a sign of the covenant between me and the earth. When I bring clouds over the earth, and the bow appears in the clouds, I will recall the covenant I have made between me and you and all living beings, so that the waters shall never again become a flood to destroy all mortal beings."

Responsorial Psalm **(Ps 25:4-5, 6-7, 8-9)**

℟. (cf. 10) Your ways, O Lord, are love and truth to those who keep your covenant.

Your ways, O LORD, make known to me;
teach me your paths,
Guide me in your truth and teach me,
for you are God my savior.

℟. Your ways, O Lord, are love and truth to those who keep your covenant.

Remember that your compassion, O LORD,
and your love are from of old.
In your kindness remember me,
because of your goodness, O LORD.

℟. Your ways, O Lord, are love and truth to those who keep your covenant.

Good and upright is the LORD,
thus he shows sinners the way.
He guides the humble to justice,
and he teaches the humble his way.

℟. Your ways, O Lord, are love and truth to those who keep your covenant.

See Appendix, p. 203, for Second Reading

Reflecting on Living the Gospel

The desert sand is not under our feet but in our hearts. Its grit is the daily irritations and indefinable loneliness we often feel. We need these Lenten weeks of heightened awareness of the importance of uncluttered spiritual and physical space where we can discover the beauty of God and our sisters and brothers under the surface sands of our busy lives. We may then become much wiser about the spiritual baggage that we, as wilderness travelers, need to keep or discard in the trek toward Easter.

Connecting the Responsorial Psalm to the Readings

The book of Genesis tells us, "[W]hen the waters had swelled on the earth for one hundred and fifty days, God remembered Noah" (7:24–8:1; NABRE) and the waters begin to subside. Today's psalm also speaks of God's remembrance: "In your kindness remember me, / because of your goodness, O Lord." In today's first reading, God offers a sign of the covenant he has made with Noah's family and with all of creation: "When I bring clouds over the earth, / and the bow appears in the clouds, / I will recall the covenant I have made."

Psalmist Preparation

At times in our lives a sign, symbol, or experience might have a profound impact on us and help call to mind our covenant with God, and with each other to live as children of God. This Lenten season, what sign or symbol might help you live more deeply into this covenant?

Prayer

God of promise,
your ways are love and truth to those who keep your covenant.
May your son, the new and everlasting covenant,
journey with us during this season of penance.
Remember your covenant and your mercies
as we strive for true and lasting holiness. Amen.

FEBRUARY 28, 2021

***Gospel* (Mark 9:2-10; L26B)**

Jesus took Peter, James, and John and led them up a high mountain apart by themselves. And he was transfigured before them, and his clothes became dazzling white, such as no fuller on earth could bleach them. Then Elijah appeared to them along with Moses, and they were conversing with Jesus. Then Peter said to Jesus in reply, "Rabbi, it is good that we are here! Let us make three tents: one for you, one for Moses, and one for Elijah." He hardly knew what to say, they were so terrified. Then a cloud came, casting a shadow over them; from the cloud came a voice, "This is my beloved Son. Listen to him." Suddenly, looking around, they no longer saw anyone but Jesus alone with them.

As they were coming down from the mountain, he charged them not to relate what they had seen to anyone, except when the Son of Man had risen from the dead. So they kept the matter to themselves, questioning what rising from the dead meant.

***First Reading* (Gen 22:1-2, 9a, 10-13, 15-18)**

God put Abraham to the test. He called to him, "Abraham!" "Here I am!" he replied. Then God said: "Take your son Isaac, your only one, whom you love, and go to the land of Moriah. There you shall offer him up as a holocaust on a height that I will point out to you."

When they came to the place of which God had told him, Abraham built an altar there and arranged the wood on it. Then he reached out and took the knife to slaughter his son. But the LORD's messenger called to him from heaven, "Abraham, Abraham!" "Here I am!" he answered. "Do not lay your hand on the boy," said the messenger. "Do not do the least thing to him. I know now how devoted you are to God, since you did not withhold from me your own beloved son." As Abraham looked about, he spied a ram caught by its horns in the thicket. So he went and took the ram and offered it up as a holocaust in place of his son.

Again the LORD's messenger called to Abraham from heaven and said: "I swear by myself, declares the LORD, that because you acted as you did in not withholding from me your beloved son, I will bless you abundantly and make your descendants as countless as the stars of the sky and the sands of the seashore; your descendants shall take possession of the gates of their enemies, and in your descendants all the nations of the earth shall find blessing—all this because you obeyed my command."

***Responsorial Psalm* (Ps 116:10, 15, 16-17, 18-19)**

℟. (116:9) I will walk before the Lord, in the land of the living.

I believed, even when I said,
"I am greatly afflicted."
Precious in the eyes of the LORD
is the death of his faithful ones.

℟. I will walk before the Lord, in the land of the living.

O LORD, I am your servant;
I am your servant, the son of your handmaid;
you have loosed my bonds.
To you will I offer sacrifice of thanksgiving,
and I will call upon the name of the LORD.

℟. I will walk before the Lord, in the land of the living.

My vows to the LORD I will pay
in the presence of all his people,
In the courts of the house of the LORD,
in your midst, O Jerusalem.

℟. I will walk before the Lord, in the land of the living.

See Appendix, p. 203, for Second Reading

Reflecting on Living the Gospel

The transfiguration is not, as some homilists state, a kind of midpoint encouragement to the disciples. The deeper meaning of the narrative for Mark and for us during Lent is that even after moments of transcendence and transformation, we must come back to earth, continue to hear the voice of Jesus, and follow him on the way to the cross. Experience of transcendence is juxtaposed with the struggle against evil. The readings today encourage deep faith and trust in God.

Connecting the Responsorial Psalm to the Readings

As Christians, we find in today's psalm response another affirmation of the resurrection promised to us in Jesus: "I will walk before the Lord, in the land of the living." A few chapters after the account of the transfiguration in Mark's gospel, Jesus will tell the Sadducees—a religious group who denied the resurrection of the dead—that God "is not God of the dead but of the living" by citing the passage in Exodus where God tells Moses, "I am the God of Abraham, [the] God of Isaac, and [the] God of Jacob" (Mark 12:26-27; NABRE).

Psalmist Preparation

Our Lenten journey will lead us to the foot of the cross and then on to the joy of the empty tomb and the waters of baptism that bring us to new birth and a life in Christ that will never end. How are you preparing yourself—body, mind, and spirit—to live these mysteries anew?

Prayer

God of holy journeys,
you are our source, you are our end,
yet you are always with us on our pilgrimage.
You urge us to *walk before the Lord, in the land of the living.*
Be with us, now and always,
that we may ever give you thanks and praise. Amen.

***Gospel* (John 2:13-25; L29B)**

Since the Passover of the Jews was near, Jesus went up to Jerusalem. He found in the temple area those who sold oxen, sheep, and doves, as well as the money changers seated there. He made a whip out of cords and drove them all out of the temple area, with the sheep and oxen, and spilled the coins of the money changers and overturned their tables, and to those who sold doves he said, "Take these out of here, and stop making my Father's house a marketplace." His disciples recalled the words of Scripture, *Zeal for your house will consume me.* At this the Jews answered and said to him, "What sign can you show us for doing this?" Jesus answered and said to them, "Destroy this temple and in three days I will raise it up." The Jews said, "This temple has been under construction for forty-six years, and you will raise it up in three days?" But he was speaking about the temple of his body. Therefore, when he was raised from the dead, his disciples remembered that he had said this, and they came to believe the Scripture and the word Jesus had spoken.

While he was in Jerusalem for the feast of Passover, many began to believe in his name when they saw the signs he was doing. But Jesus would not trust himself to them because he knew them all, and did not need anyone to testify about human nature. He himself understood it well.

***First Reading* (Exod 20:1-17 [or 20:1-3, 7-8, 12-17])**

In those days, God delivered all these commandments: "I, the Lord, am your God, who brought you out of the land of Egypt, that place of slavery. You shall not have other gods besides me. You shall not carve idols for yourselves in the shape of anything in the sky above or on the earth below or in the waters beneath the earth; you shall not bow down before them or worship them. For I, the Lord, your God, am a jealous God, inflicting punishment for their fathers' wickedness on the children of those who hate me, down to the third and fourth generation; but bestowing mercy down to the thousandth generation on the children of those who love me and keep my commandments.

"You shall not take the name of the LORD, your God, in vain. For the LORD will not leave unpunished the one who takes his name in vain.

"Remember to keep holy the sabbath day. Six days you may labor and do all your work, but the seventh day is the sabbath of the LORD, your God. No work may be done then either by you, or your son or daughter, or your male or female slave, or your beast, or by the alien who lives with you. In six days the LORD made the heavens and the earth, the sea and all that is in them; but on the seventh day he rested. That is why the LORD has blessed the sabbath day and made it holy.

"Honor your father and your mother, that you may have a long life in the land which the LORD, your God, is giving you.

You shall not kill.

You shall not commit adultery.

You shall not steal.

You shall not bear false witness against your neighbor.

You shall not covet your neighbor's house.

You shall not covet your neighbor's wife, nor his male or female slave, nor his ox or ass, nor anything else that belongs to him."

Responsorial Psalm **(Ps 19:8, 9, 10, 11)**

℟. (John 6:68c) Lord, you have the words of everlasting life.

The law of the LORD is perfect,
refreshing the soul;
The decree of the LORD is trustworthy,
giving wisdom to the simple.

℟. Lord, you have the words of everlasting life.

The precepts of the LORD are right,
rejoicing the heart;
the command of the LORD is clear,
enlightening the eye.

℟. Lord, you have the words of everlasting life.

The fear of the LORD is pure,
enduring forever;
the ordinances of the LORD are true,
all of them just.

℟. Lord, you have the words of everlasting life.

They are more precious than gold,
 than a heap of purest gold;
sweeter also than syrup
 or honey from the comb.

℟. Lord, you have the words of everlasting life.

See Appendix, p. 203, for Second Reading

Reflecting on Living the Gospel

The contemporary church cannot consider itself beyond the reach of Jesus's whip or overturning hands. When church leaders connive with unjust civil leaders, when fundraising takes precedence over faith raising, when we refuse to tolerate alternatives to religious practices and institutions, then ecclesial "cleansing" is needed by prophets driven by the Spirit of Jesus. For us who are living stones in the temple of Christ's Body, Lent is also a time for cleansing the deep personal sanctuary of our hearts, for driving out of our lives whatever clutters our discipleship.

Connecting the Responsorial Psalm to the Readings

Today's psalm is a litany of praise for the words and laws of the Lord. In their essence, the commandments given on Mount Sinai are not a restriction placed upon us, but a way that leads to the fullness of life in God's kingdom. In them we find refreshment, joy, and perfection. In the second reading from St. Paul's first letter of the Corinthians, we are told that the wisdom of the law finds its fulfillment in Jesus.

Psalmist Preparation

In the final verse of today's psalm we proclaim God's words, "They are more precious than gold, / than a heap of purest gold." These words of God contained in the Bible, and the Word of God made present in Jesus Christ, are our greatest treasure. How do you relish these gifts of God in your own life?

Prayer

God of the law, God of the prophets,
you have the words of everlasting life.
Your commands give joy to our existence,
your truths, spoken again and again, give purpose.
Make us ever attentive to your words,
especially when heard in the most surprising of places. Amen.

MARCH 14, 2021

***Gospel* (John 3:14-21; L32B)**

Jesus said to Nicodemus: "Just as Moses lifted up the serpent in the desert, so must the Son of Man be lifted up, so that everyone who believes in him may have eternal life."

For God so loved the world that he gave his only Son, so that everyone who believes in him might not perish but might have eternal life. For God did not send his Son into the world to condemn the world, but that the world might be saved through him. Whoever believes in him will not be condemned, but whoever does not believe has already been condemned, because he has not believed in the name of the only Son of God. And this is the verdict, that the light came into the world, but people preferred darkness to light, because their works were evil. For everyone who does wicked things hates the light and does not come toward the light, so that his works might not be exposed. But whoever lives the truth comes to the light, so that his works may be clearly seen as done in God.

***First Reading* (2 Chr 36:14-16, 19-23)**

In those days, all the princes of Judah, the priests, and the people added infidelity to infidelity, practicing all the abominations of the nations and polluting the LORD's temple which he had consecrated in Jerusalem.

Early and often did the LORD, the God of their fathers, send his messengers to them, for he had compassion on his people and his dwelling place. But they mocked the messengers of God, despised his warnings, and scoffed at his prophets, until the anger of the LORD against his people was so inflamed that there was no remedy. Their enemies burnt the house of God, tore down the walls of Jerusalem, set all its palaces afire, and destroyed all its precious objects. Those who escaped the sword were carried captive to Babylon, where they became servants of the king of the Chaldeans and his sons until the kingdom of the Persians came to power. All this was to fulfill the word of the LORD spoken by Jeremiah: "Until the land has retrieved its lost sabbaths, during all the time it lies waste it shall have rest while seventy years are fulfilled."

In the first year of Cyrus, king of Persia, in order to fulfill the word of the LORD spoken by Jeremiah, the LORD inspired King Cyrus of Persia to issue this proclamation throughout his kingdom, both by word of mouth and in writing: "Thus says Cyrus, king of Persia: All the kingdoms of the earth the LORD, the God of heaven, has given to me, and he has also charged me to build him a house in Jerusalem, which is in Judah. Whoever, therefore, among you belongs to any part of his people, let him go up, and may his God be with him!"

***Responsorial Psalm* (Ps 137:1-2, 3, 4-5, 6)**

℟. (6ab) Let my tongue be silenced, if I ever forget you!

By the streams of Babylon
  we sat and wept
  when we remembered Zion.
On the aspens of that land
  we hung up our harps.

℟. Let my tongue be silenced, if I ever forget you!

For there our captors asked of us
  the lyrics of our songs,
And our despoilers urged us to be joyous:
  "Sing for us the songs of Zion!"

℟. Let my tongue be silenced, if I ever forget you!

How could we sing a song of the LORD
  in a foreign land?
If I forget you, Jerusalem,
  may my right hand be forgotten!

℟. Let my tongue be silenced, if I ever forget you!

May my tongue cleave to my palate
  if I remember you not,
If I place not Jerusalem
  ahead of my joy.

℟. Let my tongue be silenced, if I ever forget you!

See Appendix, p. 203, for Second Reading

Reflecting on Living the Gospel

By visiting Jesus at night, Nicodemus avoids the daylight that might reveal him as associating with a man who is unpopular with the religious institution. To be unafraid or unashamed of professing our friendship with Jesus by the way we live always brings hard demands. We often prefer the false safety of darkness to the light of Christ that exposes, for example, our selfish, racist, sexist, or violent selves. Lent is designed to drag us out of their darkness into the Easter light of Christ through prayer, fasting, and almsgiving.

Connecting the Responsorial Psalm to the Readings

While today's first reading gives a synopsis of the Babylonian exile, the psalm gives voice to the captives' sorrow. In this time of exile the people of God enter into their faith in a new way. Though the temple has been destroyed and the holy city of Jerusalem ransacked, the people are sustained by their memories and also in the sure knowledge that their God is still with them.

Psalmist Preparation

Even in exile, the people learn how to "sing a song of the Lord / in a foreign land." What has brought you comfort in times of grief or struggle?

Prayer

God of exiles,
you yourself knew the life of refugee and stranger, fleeing a brutal and evil ruler.
In times when we feel displaced and forgotten, help us to remember to pray,
Let my tongue be silenced, if I ever forget you,
for you never forget your own. Amen.

***Gospel* (John 12:20-33; L35B)**

Some Greeks who had come to worship at the Passover Feast came to Philip, who was from Bethsaida in Galilee, and asked him, "Sir, we would like to see Jesus." Philip went and told Andrew; then Andrew and Philip went and told Jesus. Jesus answered them, "The hour has come for the Son of Man to be glorified. Amen, amen, I say to you, unless a grain of wheat falls to the ground and dies, it remains just a grain of wheat; but if it dies, it produces much fruit. Whoever loves his life loses it, and whoever hates his life in this world will preserve it for eternal life. Whoever serves me must follow me, and where I am, there also will my servant be. The Father will honor whoever serves me.

"I am troubled now. Yet what should I say? 'Father, save me from this hour'? But it was for this purpose that I came to this hour. Father, glorify your name." Then a voice came from heaven, "I have glorified it and will glorify it again." The crowd there heard it and said it was thunder; but others said, "An angel has spoken to him." Jesus answered and said, "This voice did not come for my sake but for yours. Now is the time of judgment on this world; now the ruler of this world will be driven out. And when I am lifted up from the earth, I will draw everyone to myself." He said this indicating the kind of death he would die.

***First Reading* (Jer 31:31-34)**

The days are coming, says the LORD, when I will make a new covenant with the house of Israel and the house of Judah. It will not be like the covenant I made with their fathers the day I took them by the hand to lead them forth from the land of Egypt; for they broke my covenant, and I had to show myself their master, says the LORD. But this is the covenant that I will make with the house of Israel after those days, says the LORD. I will place my law within them and write it upon their hearts; I will be their God, and they shall be my people. No longer will they have need to teach their friends and relatives how to know the LORD. All, from least to greatest, shall know me, says the LORD, for I will forgive their evildoing and remember their sin no more.

***Responsorial Psalm* (Ps 51:3-4, 12-13, 14-15)**

℟. (12a) Create a clean heart in me, O God.

Have mercy on me, O God, in your goodness;
  in the greatness of your compassion wipe out my offense.
Thoroughly wash me from my guilt
  and of my sin cleanse me.

℟. Create a clean heart in me, O God.

A clean heart create for me, O God,
  and a steadfast spirit renew within me.
Cast me not out from your presence,
  and your Holy Spirit take not from me.

℟. Create a clean heart in me, O God.

Give me back the joy of your salvation,
  and a willing spirit sustain in me.
I will teach transgressors your ways,
  and sinners shall return to you.

℟. Create a clean heart in me, O God.

See Appendix, p. 203, for Second Reading

Reflecting on Living the Gospel

Jesus tells the parable of a grain of wheat. When it is dropped into the earth, the seed "dies." But in the warmth and moisture of the earth, new life breaks out. If we wish to follow Jesus, we must empty ourselves of self-centeredness, of the instinct for self-preservation at the expense of our sisters and brothers. From seeds buried in the warm love and service of others, and watered by fidelity to our baptismal commitment, the Christian community grows into the mystery of the death and resurrection of Jesus.

Connecting the Responsorial Psalm to the Readings

The prophet Jeremiah lived during the bleakest period of Israel's history, when the southern kingdom of Judah was conquered by the Babylonians, Jerusalem and the temple destroyed, and the people taken off into exile. Today's first reading occurs near the end of the prophetic book when Jeremiah turns from condemnation to consolation. Though the people have broken the covenant time and time again, God is planning a new covenant that will be written not on stone tablets but instead upon the hearts of his people. Today's psalm implores the Lord to "[c]reate a clean heart in me, O God." This pure heart is one that is not divided by guilt, sin, or offense, but one dedicated solely to the Lord.

Psalmist Preparation

As we draw closer to Holy Week, how are you in need of God's renewing and restoring action in your heart?

Prayer

God of new beginnings,
you are goodness and compassion,
even when we believe we are undeserving.
Create a clean heart in each of us,
that we may show sinners your paths of redemption,
and labor to lead all creation back to your life and love. Amen.

PALM SUNDAY OF THE LORD'S PASSION

MARCH 28, 2021

Procession Gospel (Mark 11:1-10 [or John 12:12-16]; L37B)

Gospel (Mark 14:1–15:47 [or 15:1-39]; L38B)

First Reading **(Isa 50:4-7)**

The Lord GOD has given me
a well-trained tongue,
that I might know how to speak to the weary
a word that will rouse them.
Morning after morning
he opens my ear that I may hear;
and I have not rebelled,
have not turned back.
I gave my back to those who beat me,
my cheeks to those who plucked my beard;
my face I did not shield
from buffets and spitting.

The Lord GOD is my help,
therefore I am not disgraced;
I have set my face like flint,
knowing that I shall not be put to shame.

Responsorial Psalm **(Ps 22:8-9, 17-18, 19-20, 23-24)**

℟. (2a) My God, my God, why have you abandoned me?

All who see me scoff at me;
they mock me with parted lips, they wag their heads:
"He relied on the LORD; let him deliver him,
let him rescue him, if he loves him."

℟. My God, my God, why have you abandoned me?

Indeed, many dogs surround me,
a pack of evildoers closes in upon me;
they have pierced my hands and my feet;
I can count all my bones.

℟. My God, my God, why have you abandoned me?

They divide my garments among them,
and for my vesture they cast lots.
But you, O LORD, be not far from me;
O my help, hasten to aid me.

℟. My God, my God, why have you abandoned me?

I will proclaim your name to my brethren;
in the midst of the assembly I will praise you:
"You who fear the LORD, praise him;
all you descendants of Jacob, give glory to him;
revere him, all you descendants of Israel!"

℟. My God, my God, why have you abandoned me?

See Appendix, p. 204, for Second Reading

Reflecting on Living the Gospel

The unnamed woman's anointing of Jesus might seem a little thing, but it is the most any of us can do: she recognizes Jesus, and gives all she has for him, not understanding completely that her actions helped to prepare the King, first for his death and then for his triumph, but knowing somehow that he is the Messiah. We, too, are called to recognize Jesus the Messiah in faith, not simply as a conquering hero but as a servant willing to give himself up to death for us.

Connecting the Responsorial Psalm to the Readings

Today, we pray using the psalm that Jesus spoke on the cross: "My God, my God, why have you abandoned me?" In taking on human form, God, in the person of Jesus, took on the fullness of human experience. Being sinless did not deliver Jesus from knowing the complexities of emotion, from joy and love to grief and despair. In this psalm, however, we notice another type of death and resurrection. At the beginning, the faith of the psalmist seems to be a casualty of the peril he now finds himself in. Surrounded by his enemies, mocked and tormented, he experiences anguish that is compounded by the distance he perceives between himself and God, the deliverer. And yet, by the end of the psalm his hope has returned. He proclaims, "I will live for the Lord; / my descendants will serve you." Just as death leads to life, it seems that in the Lord despair can lead to hope.

Psalmist Preparation

The psalms embrace the fullness of human emotion, reminding us that there is nothing we cannot bring to God in prayer. How are you being called to entrust God with the whole of your life experience?

Prayer

My God, my God,
at times of desolation and anguish,
we cry to you. *Why have you abandoned me?*
Be our voice meek or strong, you hear and answer.
Help us have confidence in your eternal love of us,
and your presence with us in darkest times. Amen.

HOLY THURSDAY EVENING MASS OF THE LORD'S SUPPER

***Gospel* (John 13:1-15; L39ABC)**

Before the feast of Passover, Jesus knew that his hour had come to pass from this world to the Father. He loved his own in the world and he loved them to the end. The devil had already induced Judas, son of Simon the Iscariot, to hand him over. So, during supper, fully aware that the Father had put everything into his power and that he had come from God and was returning to God, he rose from supper and took off his outer garments. He took a towel and tied it around his waist. Then he poured water into a basin and began to wash the disciples' feet and dry them with the towel around his waist. He came to Simon Peter, who said to him, "Master, are you going to wash my feet?" Jesus answered and said to him, "What I am doing, you do not understand now, but you will understand later." Peter said to him, "You will never wash my feet." Jesus answered him, "Unless I wash you, you will have no inheritance with me." Simon Peter said to him, "Master, then not only my feet, but my hands and head as well." Jesus said to him, "Whoever has bathed has no need except to have his feet washed, for he is clean all over; so you are clean, but not all." For he knew who would betray him; for this reason, he said, "Not all of you are clean."

So when he had washed their feet and put his garments back on and reclined at table again, he said to them, "Do you realize what I have done for you? You call me 'teacher' and 'master,' and rightly so, for indeed I am. If I, therefore, the master and teacher, have washed your feet, you ought to wash one another's feet. I have given you a model to follow, so that as I have done for you, you should also do."

***First Reading* (Exod 12:1-8, 11-14)**

The LORD said to Moses and Aaron in the land of Egypt, "This month shall stand at the head of your calendar; you shall reckon it the first month of the year. Tell the whole community of Israel: On the tenth of this month every one of your families must procure for itself a lamb, one apiece for each household. If a family is too small for a whole lamb, it shall join the nearest household in procuring one and shall share in the lamb in proportion to the number of persons who partake of it. The lamb must be a year-old male and without blemish. You may take it from either the sheep or the goats. You shall keep it until the fourteenth day of this month, and then, with the whole assembly of Israel present, it shall be slaughtered during the evening twilight. They shall take some of its blood and apply it to the two doorposts and the lintel of every house in which they partake of the lamb. That same night they shall eat its roasted flesh with unleavened bread and bitter herbs.

"This is how you are to eat it: with your loins girt, sandals on your feet and your staff in hand, you shall eat like those who are in flight. It is the Passover of the LORD. For on this same night I will go through Egypt, striking down every firstborn of the land, both man and beast, and executing judgment on all the gods of Egypt—I, the LORD! But the blood will mark the houses where you are. Seeing the blood, I will pass over you; thus, when I strike the land of Egypt, no destructive blow will come upon you.

"This day shall be a memorial feast for you, which all your generations shall celebrate with pilgrimage to the LORD, as a perpetual institution."

***Responsorial Psalm* (Ps 116:12-13, 15-16bc, 17-18)**

℟. (cf. 1 Cor 10:16) Our blessing-cup is a communion with the Blood of Christ.

How shall I make a return to the LORD
for all the good he has done for me?
The cup of salvation I will take up,
and I will call upon the name of the LORD.

℟. Our blessing-cup is a communion with the Blood of Christ.

Precious in the eyes of the LORD
is the death of his faithful ones.
I am your servant, the son of your handmaid;
you have loosed my bonds.

℟. Our blessing-cup is a communion with the Blood of Christ.

To you will I offer sacrifice of thanksgiving,
and I will call upon the name of the LORD.
My vows to the LORD I will pay
in the presence of all his people.

℟. Our blessing-cup is a communion with the Blood of Christ.

See Appendix, p. 204, for Second Reading

HOLY THURSDAY EVENING MASS OF THE LORD'S SUPPER

Reflecting on Living the Gospel

Jesus's washing of his disciples' feet is the clearest expression of the Christian call to service found in all of the gospels. Jesus is explicit on this point, telling his disciples, "I have given you a model to follow, so that as I have done for you, you should also do." At the Mass of the Lord's Supper we reenact this simple yet profound gesture that reminds us of our call to serve, to wash others' feet, to do as the Master has done.

Connecting the Responsorial Psalm to the Readings

Like the second reading, today's responsorial comes from the first letter of St. Paul to the Corinthians as he recalls the institution of the Eucharist at the Last Supper. The psalm verses call to mind the paschal mystery, proclaiming, "Precious in the eyes of the Lord / is the death of his faithful ones." Our liturgy begins in joy as we sing the Gloria for the first time in many weeks and then celebrate the great gift of the Eucharist, but it ends somberly as we are invited to stay vigil with the Lord, recalling how two thousand years ago this vigil ended in arrest and eventual crucifixion.

Psalmist Preparation

This year, how is the Lord inviting you to enter deeply into the joy and sorrow of the Holy Triduum?

Prayer

Loving God,
you chose to redeem us by becoming one like us.
You know our joys, our sorrows, our pains.
In *communion with the Blood of Christ,*
may we come to know your glory, we who are your adopted sons and daughters.
Hear us when we call upon your name. Amen.

Gospel **(John 18:1–19:42; L40ABC)**

First Reading **(Isa 52:13–53:12)**

See, my servant shall prosper,
he shall be raised high and
greatly exalted.
Even as many were amazed
at him—
so marred was his look beyond
human semblance
and his appearance beyond
that of the sons of man—
so shall he startle many nations,
because of him kings shall stand speechless;
for those who have not been told shall see,
those who have not heard shall ponder it.

Who would believe what we have heard?
To whom has the arm of the LORD been revealed?
He grew up like a sapling before him,
like a shoot from the parched earth;
there was in him no stately bearing to make us look at him,
nor appearance that would attract us to him.
He was spurned and avoided by people,
a man of suffering, accustomed to infirmity,
one of those from whom people hide their faces,
spurned, and we held him in no esteem.

Yet it was our infirmities that he bore,
our sufferings that he endured,
while we thought of him as stricken,
as one smitten by God and afflicted.
But he was pierced for our offenses,
crushed for our sins;
upon him was the chastisement that makes us whole,
by his stripes we were healed.
We had all gone astray like sheep,
each following his own way;
but the LORD laid upon him
the guilt of us all.

Though he was harshly treated, he submitted
and opened not his mouth;
like a lamb led to the slaughter
or a sheep before the shearers,
he was silent and opened not his mouth.
Oppressed and condemned, he was taken away,
and who would have thought any more of his destiny?
When he was cut off from the land of the living,
and smitten for the sin of his people,
a grave was assigned him among the wicked
and a burial place with evildoers,
though he had done no wrong
nor spoken any falsehood.
But the LORD was pleased
to crush him in infirmity.

If he gives his life as an offering for sin,
he shall see his descendants in a long life,
and the will of the LORD shall be accomplished through him.

Because of his affliction
he shall see the light
in fullness of days;
through his suffering, my servant shall justify many,
and their guilt he shall bear.
Therefore I will give him his portion among the great,
and he shall divide the spoils with the mighty,
because he surrendered himself to death
and was counted among the wicked;
and he shall take away the sins of many,
and win pardon for their offenses.

***Responsorial Psalm* (Ps 31:2, 6, 12-13, 15-16, 17, 25)**

℟. (Luke 23:46) Father, into your hands I commend my spirit.

In you, O LORD, I take refuge;
let me never be put to shame.
In your justice rescue me.
Into your hands I commend my spirit;
you will redeem me, O LORD, O faithful God.

℟. Father, into your hands I commend my spirit.

For all my foes I am an object of reproach,
a laughingstock to my neighbors, and a dread to my friends;
they who see me abroad flee from me.
I am forgotten like the unremembered dead;
I am like a dish that is broken.

℟. Father, into your hands I commend my spirit.

But my trust is in you, O LORD;
I say, "You are my God.
In your hands is my destiny; rescue me
from the clutches of my enemies and my persecutors."

℟. Father, into your hands I commend my spirit.

Let your face shine upon your servant;
save me in your kindness.
Take courage and be stouthearted,
all you who hope in the LORD.

℟. Father, into your hands I commend my spirit.

See Appendix, p. 204, for Second Reading

Reflecting on Living the Gospel

Today's gospel calls us to bear witness to the profound truth that Jesus is, in fact, the Savior who died for us. The traditional hymn asks a pointed question: "Were you there when they crucified my Lord?" Each of us needs to give an answer. Are we mere spectators to the events of Good Friday or are we active participants? Where do we stand? Outside with Peter? At the foot of the cross with Mary? Or, simply among the crowd?

Connecting the Responsorial Psalm to the Readings

Today's responsorial psalm reminds us that in the midst of pain, suffering, and hardship, there is always hope, for the Lord is our "refuge" in whom we will "never be put to shame." In the responsorial we echo Jesus's words on the cross, "Father, into your hands I commend my spirit." Though all else has been taken from him in these brutal moments before death, there is one thing that cannot be taken and which Jesus gives to God as sacrifice, and also for safekeeping—his essence, his spirit.

FRIDAY OF THE LORD'S PASSION (GOOD FRIDAY)

Psalmist Preparation

Even on this most somber day of our church year, there is still Good News found in our readings. Death and destruction are not the end as the kindness of God will have the final word. How is God calling you to "take courage" today?

Prayer

Hope of all,
your son showed us that true faith in you
means aligning our will to yours:
dying each day to self, as your son died on a cross.
Into your hands this day
we give you our hearts, our souls, our very selves.
You alone are our hope. Amen.

APRIL 3, 2021

Additional readings can be found in the Lectionary for Mass.

***Gospel* (Mark 16:1-7; L41ABC)**
When the sabbath was over, Mary Magdalene, Mary, the mother of James, and Salome bought spices so that they might go and anoint him. Very early when the sun had risen, on the first day of the week, they came to the tomb. They were saying to one another, "Who will roll back the stone for us from the entrance to the tomb?" When they looked up, they saw that the stone had been rolled back; it was very large. On entering the tomb they saw a young man sitting on the right side, clothed in a white robe, and they were utterly amazed. He said to them, "Do not be amazed! You seek Jesus of Nazareth, the crucified. He has been raised; he is not here. Behold the place where they laid him. But go and tell his disciples and Peter, 'He is going before you to Galilee; there you will see him, as he told you.'"

***Epistle (Rom* 6:3-11)**
Brothers and sisters: Are you unaware that we who were baptized into Christ Jesus were baptized into his death? We were indeed buried with him through baptism into death, so that, just as Christ was raised from the dead by the glory of the Father, we too might live in newness of life.

For if we have grown into union with him through a death like his, we shall also be united with him in the resurrection. We know that our old self was crucified with him, so that our sinful body might be done away with, that we might no longer be in slavery to sin. For a dead person has been absolved from sin. If, then, we have died with Christ, we believe that we shall also live with him. We know that Christ, raised from the dead, dies no more; death no longer has power over him. As to his death, he died to sin once and for all; as to his life, he lives for God. Consequently, you too must think of yourselves as being dead to sin and living for God in Christ Jesus.

***Responsorial Psalm* (Ps 118:1-2, 16-17, 22-23)**

℟. Alleluia, alleluia, alleluia.

Give thanks to the LORD, for he is good,
for his mercy endures forever.
Let the house of Israel say,
"His mercy endures forever."

℟. Alleluia, alleluia, alleluia.

"The right hand of the LORD has struck with power;
the right hand of the LORD is exalted.
I shall not die, but live,
and declare the works of the LORD."

℟. Alleluia, alleluia, alleluia.

The stone which the builders rejected
has become the cornerstone.
By the LORD has this been done;
it is wonderful in our eyes.

℟. Alleluia, alleluia, alleluia.

Reflecting on Living the Gospel

Mark's gospel serves as an invitation that draws us ever more deeply into the paschal mystery. In this short passage, like the women who find the tomb empty and are told Jesus has been raised, we are also confronted with our own questions, with our own reactions, with our own amazement at the incredible proclamation of the resurrection of Jesus. At this liturgy, as we renew our baptismal promises, let us reaffirm anew our own Easter faith, our own Easter amazement, our own Easter joy.

Connecting the Responsorial Psalm to the Readings

Tonight we gather to relive the story of our salvation from the creation of the world to the moment of redemption when the tomb was found empty and the chains of death were crushed beneath the feet of the Lord of life. In between each of the readings we sing the ancient songs of praise, which name our God as merciful as he is mighty. Tonight's psalms call us to faithfulness and joy, as we join the saints and angels in worship that never ends.

Psalmist Preparation

At this moment in your life of faith, which of tonight's psalms speaks most directly to your heart?

Prayer

Risen Lord, *Alleluia!*
The stone which the builders rejected
has become the cornerstone.
Your re-creation permeates the entire universe;
exuberance, vitality, and vivacity surround us
and indeed take up dwelling within us.
We are an Easter people,
may our Alleluias resound loud and long! Amen.

EASTER SUNDAY OF THE RESURRECTION

***Gospel* (John 20:1-9 [or Mark 16:1-7; L41B; or Luke 24:13-35; L46]; L42ABC)**

On the first day of the week, Mary of Magdala came to the tomb early in the morning, while it was still dark, and saw the stone removed from the tomb. So she ran and went to Simon Peter and to the other disciple whom Jesus loved, and told them, "They have taken the Lord from the tomb, and we don't know where they put him." So Peter and the other disciple went out and came to the tomb. They both ran, but the other disciple ran faster than Peter and arrived at the tomb first; he bent down and saw the burial cloths there, but did not go in. When Simon Peter arrived after him, he went into the tomb and saw the burial cloths there, and the cloth that had covered his head, not with the burial cloths but rolled up in a separate place. Then the other disciple also went in, the one who had arrived at the tomb first, and he saw and believed. For they did not yet understand the Scripture that he had to rise from the dead.

***First Reading* (Acts 10:34a, 37-43)**

Peter proceeded to speak and said: "You know what has happened all over Judea, beginning in Galilee after the baptism that John preached, how God anointed Jesus of Nazareth with the Holy Spirit and power. He went about doing good and healing all those oppressed by the devil, for God was with him. We are witnesses of all that he did both in the country of the Jews and in Jerusalem. They put him to death by hanging him on a tree. This man God raised on the third day and granted that he be visible, not to all the people, but to us, the witnesses chosen by God in advance, who ate and drank with him after he rose from the dead. He commissioned us to preach to the people and testify that he is the one appointed by God as judge of the living and the dead. To him all the prophets bear witness, that everyone who believes in him will receive forgiveness of sins through his name."

***Responsorial Psalm* (Ps 118:1-2, 16-17, 22-23)**

℟. (24) This is the day the Lord has made; let us rejoice and be glad.
or: ℟. Alleluia.

Give thanks to the LORD, for he is good,
for his mercy endures forever.
Let the house of Israel say,
"His mercy endures forever."

℟. This is the day the Lord has made; let us rejoice and be glad.
or: ℟. Alleluia.

"The right hand of the LORD has struck with power;
the right hand of the LORD is exalted.
I shall not die, but live,
and declare the works of the LORD."

℟. This is the day the Lord has made; let us rejoice and be glad.
or: ℟. Alleluia.

The stone which the builders rejected
has become the cornerstone.
By the LORD has this been done;
it is wonderful in our eyes.

℟. This is the day the Lord has made; let us rejoice and be glad.
or: ℟. Alleluia.

See Appendix, p. 205, for Second Reading

Reflecting on Living the Gospel

There is an initial confusion at the empty tomb. The Beloved Disciple "saw and believed," while Peter and Mary "did not yet understand the Scripture that he had to rise from the dead." The Beloved Disciple alone initially recognizes the spiritual meaning of the empty tomb, but his understanding will soon be the foundation of the whole church, spurred by later encounters with the risen Lord. The resurrection of Jesus became the central message of the new community of disciples, and ours.

Connecting the Responsorial Psalm to the Readings

Today's psalm calls us to rejoicing and gladness as we proclaim the sure hope that "[we] shall not die, but live, / and declare the works of the

Lord." This is true at all times of the year, but at Easter we set aside a season for pure celebration as we contemplate the wonder of life that comes from death and light that banishes darkness.

Psalmist Preparation

Just as Simon Peter and the Beloved Disciple in today's gospel do not "yet understand the Scripture / that he had to rise from the dead," there is much that is still mysterious and hidden to us about the Lord's resurrection. During this Easter season how will you live into the joy of the paschal mystery while meditating on the identity of the one who is the Lord of life?

Prayer

God of the empty tomb,
today, the eighth day, the world is created anew!
This is the day made new by your resurrection, *let us rejoice and be glad.*
Let alleluias ring forth like bells, and may our song never cease.
This is the feast of victory! Amen.

SECOND SUNDAY OF EASTER (OR OF DIVINE MERCY)

APRIL 11, 2021

Gospel (John 20:19-31; L44B)

On the evening of that first day of the week, when the doors were locked, where the disciples were, for fear of the Jews, Jesus came and stood in their midst and said to them, "Peace be with you." When he had said this, he showed them his hands and his side. The disciples rejoiced when they saw the Lord. Jesus said to them again, "Peace be with you. As the Father has sent me, so I send you." And when he had said this, he breathed on them and said to them, "Receive the Holy Spirit. Whose sins you forgive are forgiven them, and whose sins you retain are retained."

Thomas, called Didymus, one of the Twelve, was not with them when Jesus came. So the other disciples said to him, "We have seen the Lord." But he said to them, "Unless I see the mark of the nails in his hands and put my finger into the nailmarks and put my hand into his side, I will not believe."

Now a week later his disciples were again inside and Thomas was with them. Jesus came, although the doors were locked, and stood in their midst and said, "Peace be with you." Then he said to Thomas, "Put your finger here and see my hands, and bring your hand and put it into my side, and do not be unbelieving, but believe." Thomas answered and said to him, "My Lord and my God!" Jesus said to him, "Have you come to believe because you have seen me? Blessed are those who have not seen and have believed."

Now Jesus did many other signs in the presence of his disciples that are not written in this book. But these are written that you may come to believe that Jesus is the Christ, the Son of God, and that through this belief you may have life in his name.

First Reading (Acts 4:32-35)

The community of believers was of one heart and mind, and no one claimed that any of his possessions was his own, but they had everything in common. With great power the apostles bore witness to the resurrection of the Lord Jesus, and great favor was accorded them all. There was no needy person among them, for those who owned property or houses would sell them, bring the proceeds of the sale, and put them at the feet of the apostles, and they were distributed to each according to need.

***Responsorial Psalm* (Ps 118:2-4, 13-15, 22-24)**

℟. (1) Give thanks to the Lord for he is good, his love is everlasting.
or: ℟. Alleluia.

Let the house of Israel say,
"His mercy endures forever."
Let the house of Aaron say,
"His mercy endures forever."
Let those who fear the LORD say,
"His mercy endures forever."

℟. Give thanks to the Lord for he is good, his love is everlasting.
or: ℟. Alleluia.

I was hard pressed and was falling,
but the LORD helped me.
My strength and my courage is the LORD,
and he has been my savior.
The joyful shout of victory
in the tents of the just.

℟. Give thanks to the Lord for he is good, his love is everlasting.
or: ℟. Alleluia.

The stone which the builders rejected
has become the cornerstone.
By the LORD has this been done;
it is wonderful in our eyes.
This is the day the LORD has made;
let us be glad and rejoice in it.

℟. Give thanks to the Lord for he is good, his love is everlasting.
or: ℟. Alleluia.

See Appendix, p. 205, for Second Reading

Reflecting on Living the Gospel

Christ took his wounds into the grave and did not disown them in his resurrection. Because of his wounds, Jesus is now in touch with wounded humanity: those wounded in body and spirit, those hurt by society, victims of violence, those suffering from their own addictions, those abused by our disregard and complacency. And we each know only too well our own woundedness. Such wounds reveal our need for one another and the potential for building a compassionate, healing community that witnesses to the love of the Wounded Healer.

Connecting the Responsorial Psalm to the Readings

Aptly, on this feast of Divine Mercy, today's responsorial psalm repeats three times, "His mercy endures forever." In the gospel reading Jesus embodies the mercy of God, drawing near to those who had abandoned him in his greatest suffering with the words, "Peace be with you." Jesus does not rebuke the disciples for their lack of faith or wait for them to seek him out. Instead, he passes through the doors they had locked out of fear and greets them as friends. For their part we are told, "The disciples rejoiced when they saw the Lord."

Psalmist Preparation

God's eternal mercy also calls us to joy. How do you express this joy in your ministry?

Prayer

Merciful God,
your compassion is nowhere more present than in your son,
risen from the tomb: *his love is everlasting.*
May we echo on earth all that you have given us,
and may we, by holding steadfast to your law of love,
help make your salvation known to all. Amen.

***Gospel* (Luke 24:35-48; L47B)**

The two disciples recounted what had taken place on the way, and how Jesus was made known to them in the breaking of bread.

While they were still speaking about this, he stood in their midst and said to them, "Peace be with you." But they were startled and terrified and thought that they were seeing a ghost. Then he said to them, "Why are you troubled? And why do questions arise in your hearts? Look at my hands and my feet, that it is I myself. Touch me and see, because a ghost does not have flesh and bones as you can see I have." And as he said this, he showed them his hands and his feet. While they were still incredulous for joy and were amazed, he asked them, "Have you anything here to eat?" They gave him a piece of baked fish; he took it and ate it in front of them.

He said to them, "These are my words that I spoke to you while I was still with you, that everything written about me in the law of Moses and in the prophets and psalms must be fulfilled." Then he opened their minds to understand the Scriptures. And he said to them, "Thus it is written that the Christ would suffer and rise from the dead on the third day and that repentance, for the forgiveness of sins, would be preached in his name to all the nations, beginning from Jerusalem. You are witnesses of these things."

***First Reading* (Acts 3:13-15, 17-19)**

Peter said to the people: "The God of Abraham, the God of Isaac, and the God of Jacob, the God of our fathers, has glorified his servant Jesus, whom you handed over and denied in Pilate's presence when he had decided to release him. You denied the Holy and Righteous One and asked that a murderer be released to you. The author of life you put to death, but God raised him from the dead; of this we are witnesses. Now I know, brothers, that you acted out of ignorance, just as your leaders did; but God has thus brought to fulfillment what he had announced beforehand through the mouth of all the prophets, that his Christ would suffer. Repent, therefore, and be converted, that your sins may be wiped away."

***Responsorial Psalm* (Ps 4:2, 4, 7-8, 9)**

℟. (7a) Lord, let your face shine on us. *or:* ℟. Alleluia.

When I call, answer me, O my just God,
you who relieve me when I am in distress;
have pity on me, and hear my prayer!

℟. Lord, let your face shine on us. *or:* ℟. Alleluia.

Know that the LORD does wonders for his faithful one;
the LORD will hear me when I call upon him.

℟. Lord, let your face shine on us. *or:* ℟. Alleluia.

O LORD, let the light of your countenance shine upon us!
You put gladness into my heart.

℟. Lord, let your face shine on us. *or:* ℟. Alleluia.

As soon as I lie down, I fall peacefully asleep,
for you alone, O LORD,
bring security to my dwelling.

℟. Lord, let your face shine on us. *or:* ℟. Alleluia.

See Appendix, p. 205, for Second Reading

Reflecting on Living the Gospel

Jesus's passion and resurrection transformed the table of Jesus the prophet into that of Jesus Christ the Lord and made it the springboard for the church's universal mission. If we are to be disciples who take seriously Jesus's Easter greeting of "Peace be with you!" and who offer this peace to one another around the eucharistic table, we need to create a space in our lives and our hearts where such peace with God and with our sisters and brothers can truly be at home.

Connecting the Responsorial Psalm to the Readings

Today's psalm exhorts us to trust in "the LORD [who] does wonders for his faithful one." In speaking to the gathered crowd, Peter calls upon "[t]he God of Abraham, the God of Isaac, and the God of Jacob, / the God of our fathers." Throughout the generations we see the mighty works of the Lord in our biblical ancestors and hear about them in the stories told in our communities and families about the saints among us. Though the first verse speaks of "distress" and the need for "pity" from God, the next verses express faith that "the Lord will hear me when I call upon him" and names God as the one who puts "gladness into my heart."

Psalmist Preparation

The holy men and women we look to as models in the life of faith show us how to praise God even in the midst of hardship. How do you attempt to do this in your own life?

Prayer

God of glories,
just as Peter, James, and John
once saw you radiant in glory on the hilltop,
let your face shine on us.
At the altar, give to us a glimpse of your eternal reign,
a foretaste of the heavenly banquet,
in food that is you, Lord, forever and ever. Amen.

APRIL 25, 2021

***Gospel* (John 10:11-18; L50B)**

Jesus said: "I am the good shepherd. A good shepherd lays down his life for the sheep. A hired man, who is not a shepherd and whose sheep are not his own, sees a wolf coming and leaves the sheep and runs away, and the wolf catches and scatters them. This is because he works for pay and has no concern for the sheep. I am the good shepherd, and I know mine and mine know me, just as the Father knows me and I know the Father; and I will lay down my life for the sheep. I have other sheep that do not belong to this fold. These also I must lead, and they will hear my voice, and there will be one flock, one shepherd. This is why the Father loves me, because I lay down my life in order to take it up again. No one takes it from me, but I lay it down on my own. I have power to lay it down, and power to take it up again. This command I have received from my Father."

***First Reading* (Acts 4:8-12)**

Peter, filled with the Holy Spirit, said: "Leaders of the people and elders: If we are being examined today about a good deed done to a cripple, namely, by what means he was saved, then all of you and all the people of Israel should know that it was in the name of Jesus Christ the Nazorean whom you crucified, whom God raised from the dead; in his name this man stands before you healed. He is *the stone rejected by you, the builders, which has become the cornerstone.* There is no salvation through anyone else, nor is there any other name under heaven given to the human race by which we are to be saved."

***Responsorial Psalm* (Ps 118:1, 8-9, 21-23, 26, 28, 29)**

℟. (22) The stone rejected by the builders has become the cornerstone.
or: ℟. Alleluia.

Give thanks to the LORD, for he is good,
  for his mercy endures forever.
It is better to take refuge in the LORD
  than to trust in man.
It is better to take refuge in the LORD
  than to trust in princes.

℟. The stone rejected by the builders has become the cornerstone.
or: ℟. Alleluia.

I will give thanks to you, for you have answered me
  and have been my savior.
The stone which the builders rejected
  has become the cornerstone.
By the LORD has this been done;
  it is wonderful in our eyes.

℟. The stone rejected by the builders has become the cornerstone.
or: ℟. Alleluia.

Blessed is he who comes in the name of the LORD;
  we bless you from the house of the LORD.
I will give thanks to you, for you have answered me
  and have been my savior.
Give thanks to the LORD, for he is good;
  for his kindness endures forever.

℟. The stone rejected by the builders has become the cornerstone.
or: ℟. Alleluia.

See Appendix, p. 205, for Second Reading

Reflecting on Living the Gospel
As our Good Shepherd, Jesus fights for us, saves us from the gaping jaws of whatever or whoever seeks to grab and destroy our discipleship and wound the "little flock" of the Christian community. He shepherds us with his loving care. In contrast is the hireling who is concerned primarily with his own self-interest: his reputation, remuneration, and

safety. There are still some political, social, and ecclesial "hired men" with us, but there are also the magnificent shepherds who are willing to lay down their life for their sheep.

Connecting the Responsorial Psalm to the Readings

Today's psalm tells us, "Blessed is he who comes in the name of the Lord." We see this lived out in the experiences of Peter and John in the Acts of the Apostles. Filled with the grace of the Holy Spirit newly descended upon them, the two apostles heal a crippled man, stating, "[I]n the name of Jesus Christ the Nazorean, [rise and] walk" (Acts 3:6; NABRE). In today's first reading, their faith does not falter as they are brought before the Sanhedrin due to the crowd's excitement about this healing and about Peter's preaching afterward. In blessing they healed the man, and as *the* blessed they have courage and peace in defending their faith before those who had recently succeeded in bringing Jesus to the cross.

Psalmist Preparation

As a cantor, how do you experience your ministry as a blessing done "in the name of the Lord"?

Prayer

Stone rejected by the builders,
we too at times feel abandoned, cast aside.
Help us remember that you are our cornerstone,
a solid foundation of faith, church, and community.
Give us strong voices to ever praise your name,
here in your holy house, and everywhere we may go. Amen.

***Gospel* (John 15:1-8; L53B)**
Jesus said to his disciples: "I am the true vine, and my Father is the vine grower. He takes away every branch in me that does not bear fruit, and every one that does he prunes so that it bears more fruit. You are already pruned because of the word that I spoke to you. Remain in me, as I remain in you. Just as a branch cannot bear fruit on its own unless it remains on the vine, so neither can you unless you remain in me. I am the vine, you are the branches. Whoever remains in me and I in him will bear much fruit, because without me you can do nothing. Anyone who does not remain in me will be thrown out like a branch and wither; people will gather them and throw them into a fire and they will be burned. If you remain in me and my words remain in you, ask for whatever you want and it will be done for you. By this is my Father glorified, that you bear much fruit and become my disciples."

***First Reading* (Acts 9:26-31)**
When Saul arrived in Jerusalem he tried to join the disciples, but they were all afraid of him, not believing that he was a disciple. Then Barnabas took charge of him and brought him to the apostles, and he reported to them how he had seen the Lord, and that he had spoken to him, and how in Damascus he had spoken out boldly in the name of Jesus. He moved about freely with them in Jerusalem, and spoke out boldly in the name of the Lord. He also spoke and debated with the Hellenists, but they tried to kill him. And when the brothers learned of this, they took him down to Caesarea and sent him on his way to Tarsus.

The church throughout all Judea, Galilee, and Samaria was at peace. It was being built up and walked in the fear of the Lord, and with the consolation of the Holy Spirit it grew in numbers.

***Responsorial Psalm* (Ps 22:26-27, 28, 30, 31-32)**

℟. (26a) I will praise you, Lord, in the assembly of your people.
or: ℟. Alleluia.

I will fulfill my vows before those who fear the LORD.
The lowly shall eat their fill;
they who seek the LORD shall praise him:
"May your hearts live forever!"

℟. I will praise you, Lord, in the assembly of your people.
or: ℟. Alleluia.

All the ends of the earth
shall remember and turn to the LORD;
all the families of the nations
shall bow down before him.

℟. I will praise you, Lord, in the assembly of your people.
or: ℟. Alleluia.

To him alone shall bow down
all who sleep in the earth;
before him shall bend
all who go down into the dust.

℟. I will praise you, Lord, in the assembly of your people.
or: ℟. Alleluia.

And to him my soul shall live;
my descendants shall serve him.
Let the coming generation be told of the LORD
that they may proclaim to a people yet to be born
the justice he has shown.

℟. I will praise you, Lord, in the assembly of your people.
or: ℟. Alleluia.

See Appendix, p. 206, for Second Reading

Reflecting on Living the Gospel

To remain healthy and productive a vine must be pruned. We must accept not only the short, sharp pain of our vine-grower God snipping from our lives the small and withering infidelities, but also the longer agony of more drastic pruning that is sometimes necessary. Sometimes God recognizes our potential for greater fruit-bearing, and with this the need for heavy pruning. After such pruning, a vine may bear no fruit for several years, waiting and confident in the tending of the Vine Grower, until both are rewarded with a tremendous, bursting yield.

Connecting the Responsorial Psalm to the Readings

In today's first reading we continue on with the saga of the early church recorded in the Acts of the Apostles, this time focusing on Paul's journey of faith. In a shocking and dramatic conversion, Paul goes from persecutor of Christians to an apostle of Jesus. Though the other apostles are first afraid to accept him into their midst, they are finally convinced of his change of heart when they hear stories and witness his bold preaching "in the name of the Lord." The responsorial psalm is an apt description of Paul, eager to praise the Lord "in the assembly of your people." We can imagine Paul praying the final verse, "[T]o him my soul shall live," as he dedicates his life to preaching the Gospel and sharing with others the salvation he has received.

Psalmist Preparation

Within the assembly of God's people, you are blessed to proclaim the praises of the Lord. At this moment in time, where do you find the most joy in your ministry?

Prayer

God of all nations,
you give food to the lowly,
safety to the insecure, shelter to the homeless.
All the ends of the earth will praise you
not only *in the assembly of your people*
but throughout the land:
you have saved and set us free! Amen.

MAY 9, 2021

***Gospel* (John 15:9-17; L56B)**

Jesus said to his disciples: "As the Father loves me, so I also love you. Remain in my love. If you keep my commandments, you will remain in my love, just as I have kept my Father's commandments and remain in his love.

"I have told you this so that my joy may be in you and your joy might be complete. This is my commandment: love one another as I love you. No one has greater love than this, to lay down one's life for one's friends. You are my friends if you do what I command you. I no longer call you slaves, because a slave does not know what his master is doing. I have called you friends, because I have told you everything I have heard from my Father. It was not you who chose me, but I who chose you and appointed you to go and bear fruit that will remain, so that whatever you ask the Father in my name he may give you. This I command you: love one another."

***First Reading* (Acts 10:25-26, 34-35, 44-48)**

When Peter entered, Cornelius met him and, falling at his feet, paid him homage. Peter, however, raised him up, saying, "Get up. I myself am also a human being."

Then Peter proceeded to speak and said, "In truth, I see that God shows no partiality. Rather, in every nation whoever fears him and acts uprightly is acceptable to him."

While Peter was still speaking these things, the Holy Spirit fell upon all who were listening to the word. The circumcised believers who had accompanied Peter were astounded that the gift of the Holy Spirit should have been poured out on the Gentiles also, for they could hear them speaking in tongues and glorifying God. Then Peter responded, "Can anyone withhold the water for baptizing these people, who have received the Holy Spirit even as we have?" He ordered them to be baptized in the name of Jesus Christ.

Responsorial Psalm **(Ps 98:1, 2-3, 3-4)**

℟. (cf. 2b) The Lord has revealed to the nations his saving power.
or: ℟. Alleluia.

Sing to the LORD a new song,
  for he has done wondrous deeds;
His right hand has won victory for him,
  his holy arm.

℟. The Lord has revealed to the nations his saving power.
or: ℟. Alleluia.

The LORD has made his salvation known:
  in the sight of the nations he has revealed his justice.
He has remembered his kindness and his faithfulness
  toward the house of Israel.

℟. The Lord has revealed to the nations his saving power.
or: ℟. Alleluia.

All the ends of the earth have seen
  the salvation by our God.
Sing joyfully to the LORD, all you lands;
  break into song; sing praise.

℟. The Lord has revealed to the nations his saving power.
or: ℟. Alleluia.

See Appendix, p. 206, for Second Reading

Reflecting on Living the Gospel

One of the most priceless human gifts is friendship. It allows us to disclose ourselves to and receive from another in complete openness and trust. With a friend we can think aloud; participate in one another's joys and sorrows, hopes and fears; survive loneliness, indifference, hostility. Small wonder, then, that in today's gospel Jesus calls his disciples by this most precious of names: "my friends." Drawn into and abiding in the mutual love of the Father and the Son, disciples are no longer called servants but friends.

Connecting the Responsorial Psalm to the Readings

Today's psalm invokes us to "[s]ing to the LORD a new song." Peter's actions in the Acts of the Apostles lead to a new age in the life of the church and within the history of salvation as both Jews and Gentiles join together in Jesus to praise and worship the living God.

Psalmist Preparation

St. Augustine famously addressed God as the one who is "ever ancient, ever new." Our faith calls us to a dynamic tension between these seemingly opposing truths of our Creator, and away from statically clinging to tradition when God is calling us to newness in the spiritual life. Where is your community being challenged to "sing to the LORD a new song"?

Prayer

Wondrous Savior,
you have, throughout all time, *revealed to the nations saving power:*
mighty deeds in the days of former covenants,
and a mighty redeemer in your son, Jesus Christ.
We sing to you a song ever-ancient and ever-new:
Alleluia! We praise your name. Amen.

***Gospel* (Mark 16:15-20; L58B)**

Jesus said to his disciples: "Go into the whole world and proclaim the gospel to every creature. Whoever believes and is baptized will be saved; whoever does not believe will be condemned. These signs will accompany those who believe: in my name they will drive out demons, they will speak new languages. They will pick up serpents with their hands, and if they drink any deadly thing, it will not harm them. They will lay hands on the sick, and they will recover."

So then the Lord Jesus, after he spoke to them, was taken up into heaven and took his seat at the right hand of God. But they went forth and preached everywhere, while the Lord worked with them and confirmed the word through accompanying signs.

***First Reading* (Acts 1:1-11)**

In the first book, Theophilus, I dealt with all that Jesus did and taught until the day he was taken up, after giving instructions through the Holy Spirit to the apostles whom he had chosen. He presented himself alive to them by many proofs after he had suffered, appearing to them during forty days and speaking about the kingdom of God. While meeting with them, he enjoined them not to depart from Jerusalem, but to wait for "the promise of the Father about which you have heard me speak; for John baptized with water, but in a few days you will be baptized with the Holy Spirit."

When they had gathered together they asked him, "Lord, are you at this time going to restore the kingdom to Israel?" He answered them, "It is not for you to know the times or seasons that the Father has established by his own authority. But you will receive power when the Holy Spirit comes upon you, and you will be my witnesses in Jerusalem, throughout Judea and Samaria, and to the ends of the earth." When he had said this, as they were looking on, he was lifted up, and a cloud took him from their sight. While they were looking intently at the sky as he was going, suddenly two men dressed in white garments stood beside them. They said, "Men of Galilee, why are you standing there looking at the sky? This Jesus who has been taken up from you into heaven will return in the same way as you have seen him going into heaven."

***Responsorial Psalm* (Ps 47:2-3, 6-7, 8-9)**

℟. (6) God mounts his throne to shouts of joy: a blare of trumpets for the Lord. *or:* ℟. Alleluia.

All you peoples, clap your hands,
shout to God with cries of gladness,
for the LORD, the Most High, the awesome,
is the great king over all the earth.

℟. God mounts his throne to shouts of joy: a blare of trumpets for the Lord. *or:* ℟. Alleluia.

God mounts his throne amid shouts of joy;
the LORD, amid trumpet blasts.
Sing praise to God, sing praise;
sing praise to our king, sing praise.

℟. God mounts his throne to shouts of joy: a blare of trumpets for the Lord. *or:* ℟. Alleluia.

For king of all the earth is God;
sing hymns of praise.
God reigns over the nations,
God sits upon his holy throne.

℟. God mounts his throne to shouts of joy: a blare of trumpets for the Lord. *or:* ℟. Alleluia.

See Appendix, p. 206, for Second Reading

Reflecting on Living the Gospel

Like the Eleven, we are also people entrusted with the mission of proclaiming the Gospel now that Jesus has ascended to heaven and is no longer with us physically. We too are sent to do new wonders, speak new words with the fire of the Spirit on our tongues, offer new healing to our sisters and brothers, and cast out contemporary "demons" from ourselves and others. And all this continues to be "in the name of," in the personal power of Jesus into whose Body we are baptized.

Connecting the Responsorial Psalm to the Readings

The wonders of the risen Lord continue to astonish and amaze the apostles. Not only has Jesus overcome the finality of death, now he is "taken up into heaven" where he "[takes] his seat at the right hand of God." Today's psalm is an apt response for those first apostles, and also for us modern-day disciples, as we reflect on the mystery of the ascension. The psalmist sings, "For the Lord, the Most High, the awesome, / is the great king over all the earth." Due to its everyday use, the term "awesome" might have begun to lose its significance for most of us. Literally, the word means "to inspire awe." Biblically, we can see it as one of the gifts of the Holy Spirit, "awe and wonder," which is sometimes translated as "fear of the Lord."

Psalmist Preparation

How do you seek to cultivate a sense of awe and wonder in your own life and especially when encountering the divine?

Prayer

God who reigns,
a blare of trumpets announces your majesty,
shouts of joy accompany you on your heavenly throne.
In gladness we begin to live our lives the way you lived while on earth:
healing, preaching, bringing forth your kingdom.
May your return not be too distant. Amen.

MAY 16, 2021

***Gospel* (John 17:11b-19; L60B)**

Lifting up his eyes to heaven, Jesus prayed, saying: "Holy Father, keep them in your name that you have given me, so that they may be one just as we are one. When I was with them I protected them in your name that you gave me, and I guarded them, and none of them was lost except the son of destruction, in order that the Scripture might be fulfilled. But now I am coming to you. I speak this in the world so that they may share my joy completely. I gave them your word, and the world hated them, because they do not belong to the world any more than I belong to the world. I do not ask that you take them out of the world but that you keep them from the evil one. They do not belong to the world any more than I belong to the world. Consecrate them in the truth. Your word is truth. As you sent me into the world, so I sent them into the world. And I consecrate myself for them, so that they also may be consecrated in truth."

***First Reading* (Acts 1:15-17, 20a, 20c-26)**

Peter stood up in the midst of the brothers—there was a group of about one hundred and twenty persons in the one place—. He said, "My brothers, the Scripture had to be fulfilled which the Holy Spirit spoke beforehand through the mouth of David, concerning Judas, who was the guide for those who arrested Jesus. He was numbered among us and was allotted a share in this ministry.

"For it is written in the Book of Psalms:

May another take his office.

"Therefore, it is necessary that one of the men who accompanied us the whole time the Lord Jesus came and went among us, beginning from the baptism of John until the day on which he was taken up from us, become with us a witness to his resurrection." So they proposed two, Judas called Barsabbas, who was also known as Justus, and Matthias. Then they prayed, "You, Lord, who know the hearts of all, show which one of these two you have chosen to take the place in this apostolic ministry from which Judas turned away to go to his own place." Then they gave lots to them, and the lot fell upon Matthias, and he was counted with the eleven apostles.

***Responsorial Psalm* (Ps 103:1-2, 11-12, 19-20)**

℟. (19a) The Lord has set his throne in heaven. *or:* ℟. Alleluia.

Bless the LORD, O my soul;
and all my being, bless his holy name.
Bless the LORD, O my soul,
and forget not all his benefits.

℟. The Lord has set his throne in heaven. *or:* ℟. Alleluia.

For as the heavens are high above the earth,
so surpassing is his kindness toward those who fear him.
As far as the east is from the west,
so far has he put our transgressions from us.

℟. The Lord has set his throne in heaven. *or:* ℟. Alleluia.

The LORD has established his throne in heaven,
and his kingdom rules over all.
Bless the LORD, all you his angels,
you mighty in strength, who do his bidding.

℟. The Lord has set his throne in heaven. *or:* ℟. Alleluia.

See Appendix, p. 207, for Second Reading

Reflecting on Living the Gospel

The readings for this Sunday before Pentecost provide a bridge between the continued celebration of the resurrection and yearning for God's Spirit, which will come only after the departure of Jesus. Jesus's prayer anticipates the coming of the Spirit of truth (14:7; 15:26). Today—after years of deplorable accounts of sexual and financial abuse in the church—this final wish of Jesus that his Father make the church holy in truth has a dramatic relevance.

Connecting the Responsorial Psalm to the Readings

Today's psalm proclaims, "As far as the east is from the west, / so far has he put our transgressions from us." As human beings we will falter and stumble on the journey of faith, and yet we are assured of our God's tender love and infinite compassion. We know that as God has done, so we are called to do. In today's gospel Jesus prays that his disciples might be bonded together in unity, filled with complete joy, and "consecrated in truth." All these become possible when we extend the same mercy to others that God has extended to us.

Psalmist Preparation

How might God be calling you to practice forgiveness at this moment in your life?

Prayer

Lord,
from your *throne in heaven* you bless us with kindness and forgiveness.
Grant us also apostolic zeal,
that the whole world may come to know your Good News by all we say and do.
We make this prayer through Christ our Lord. Amen.

***Gospel* (John 20:19-23 [or John 15:26-27; 16:12-15]; L63B)**

On the evening of that first day of the week, when the doors were locked, where the disciples were, for fear of the Jews, Jesus came and stood in their midst and said to them, "Peace be with you." When he had said this, he showed them his hands and his side. The disciples rejoiced when they saw the Lord. Jesus said to them again, "Peace be with you. As the Father has sent me, so I send you." And when he had said this, he breathed on them and said to them, "Receive the Holy Spirit. Whose sins you forgive are forgiven them, and whose sins you retain are retained."

First Reading (Acts 2:1-11)

When the time for Pentecost was fulfilled, they were all in one place together. And suddenly there came from the sky a noise like a strong driving wind, and it filled the entire house in which they were. Then there appeared to them tongues as of fire, which parted and came to rest on each one of them. And they were all filled with the Holy Spirit and began to speak in different tongues, as the Spirit enabled them to proclaim.

Now there were devout Jews from every nation under heaven staying in Jerusalem. At this sound, they gathered in a large crowd, but they were confused because each one heard them speaking in his own language. They were astounded, and in amazement they asked, "Are not all these people who are speaking Galileans? Then how does each of us hear them in his native language? We are Parthians, Medes, and Elamites, inhabitants of Mesopotamia, Judea and Cappadocia, Pontus and Asia, Phrygia and Pamphylia, Egypt and the districts of Libya near Cyrene, as well as travelers from Rome, both Jews and converts to Judaism, Cretans and Arabs, yet we hear them speaking in our own tongues of the mighty acts of God."

***Responsorial Psalm* (Ps 104:1, 24, 29-30, 31, 34)**

℟. (cf. 30) Lord, send out your Spirit, and renew the face of the earth.
or: ℟. Alleluia.

Bless the LORD, O my soul!
O LORD, my God, you are great indeed!
How manifold are your works, O LORD!
The earth is full of your creatures.

℟. Lord, send out your Spirit, and renew the face of the earth.
or: ℟. Alleluia.

If you take away their breath, they perish
and return to their dust.
When you send forth your spirit, they are created,
and you renew the face of the earth.

℟. Lord, send out your Spirit, and renew the face of the earth.
or: ℟. Alleluia.

May the glory of the LORD endure forever;
may the LORD be glad in his works!
Pleasing to him be my theme;
I will be glad in the LORD.

℟. Lord, send out your Spirit, and renew the face of the earth.
or: ℟. Alleluia.

See Appendix, p. 207, for Second Reading

Reflecting on Living the Gospel

Now Christ "sends" his disciples. He gives them a mission, that of forgiving sins. Since, however, Christ draws a parallel between his action in sending the disciples and the Father's action in sending him, he is also telling the disciples that they are to continue the work that Jesus himself has been doing for the reconstruction of the world. They too are to do the Father's work. As Jesus reveals the Father and makes him known, so the disciples are to reveal Jesus and make him known.

Connecting the Responsorial Psalm to the Readings

Today's psalm lifts up another aspect of the Holy Spirit as an agent of renewal in the world. Within the life of creation, we see a pattern of death and rebirth constantly at work. For those of us living in the Northern Hemisphere, we celebrate the Easter season during a time where new life is appearing all around us in the form of plants and newborn birds and animals. Following the dark and cold of the winter months, the warmth and light of spring reminds us that our creator God is constantly at work "renew[ing] the face of the earth."

Psalmist Preparation

How are you experiencing or in need of the Holy Spirit's renewing action in your own life right now?

Prayer

Spirit of God,
come, be with us and be within us.
Come, give new life to us, *and renew the face of the earth.*
Be our very breath, the breath that created the world
and enlivened Adam and Eve.
Be a wind of change and promise in our lives. Amen.

MAY 30, 2021

***Gospel* (Matt 28:16-20; L165B)**

The eleven disciples went to Galilee, to the mountain to which Jesus had ordered them. When they all saw him, they worshiped, but they doubted. Then Jesus approached and said to them, "All power in heaven and on earth has been given to me. Go, therefore, and make disciples of all nations, baptizing them in the name of the Father, and of the Son, and of the Holy Spirit, teaching them to observe all that I have commanded you. And behold, I am with you always, until the end of the age."

***First Reading* (Deut 4:32-34, 39-40)**

Moses said to the people: "Ask now of the days of old, before your time, ever since God created man upon the earth; ask from one end of the sky to the other: Did anything so great ever happen before? Was it ever heard of? Did a people ever hear the voice of God speaking from the midst of fire, as you did, and live? Or did any god venture to go and take a nation for himself from the midst of another nation, by testings, by signs and wonders, by war, with strong hand and outstretched arm, and by great terrors, all of which the LORD, your God, did for you in Egypt before your very eyes? This is why you must now know, and fix in your heart, that the LORD is God in the heavens above and on earth below, and that there is no other. You must keep his statutes and commandments that I enjoin on you today, that you and your children after you may prosper, and that you may have long life on the land which the LORD, your God, is giving you forever."

***Responsorial Psalm* (Ps 33:4-5, 6, 9, 18-19, 20, 22)**

℟. (12b) Blessed the people the Lord has chosen to be his own.

Upright is the word of the LORD,
 and all his works are trustworthy.
He loves justice and right;
 of the kindness of the LORD the earth is full.

℟. Blessed the people the Lord has chosen to be his own.

By the word of the LORD the heavens were made;
by the breath of his mouth all their host.
For he spoke, and it was made;
he commanded, and it stood forth.

℟. Blessed the people the Lord has chosen to be his own.

See, the eyes of the LORD are upon those who fear him,
upon those who hope for his kindness,
To deliver them from death
and preserve them in spite of famine.

℟. Blessed the people the Lord has chosen to be his own.

Our soul waits for the LORD,
who is our help and our shield.
May your kindness, O LORD, be upon us
who have put our hope in you.

℟. Blessed the people the Lord has chosen to be his own.

See Appendix, p. 207, for Second Reading

Reflecting on Living the Gospel

Matthew gives us the solemn assurance that Jesus, "God-with-us" (cf. Matt 1:23), will be with the church until the end of history. His is no "absentee lordship" but a presence of a servant Christ who wishes to liberate rather than dominate. His church must also be a humble servant that remembers its authority is not absolute but derived from Jesus; a church that identifies with those who are a very human mix of faith and doubt; a church that avoids all triumphalism and insensitivity to the wounded people of our world.

Connecting the Responsorial Psalm to the Readings

Today's psalm proclaims "of the kindness of the Lord the earth is full." As Christians, we experience the fullness of God through the mystery of the Most Holy Trinity. We understand God as Father, Son, and Holy Spirit to be a relationship of love that overflows to animate all of creation. Through this love we have been chosen to be God's own and to also care for and steward the abundance of creation. In the first reading, our thriving is linked to keeping the "statutes and commandments" of God, for in this way, Moses tells the people, "[Y]ou and your children after you may prosper, / and [you will] have long life on the land / which the Lord, your God, is giving you forever."

Psalmist Preparation
How do you make care and enjoyment of creation part of your spiritual life?

Prayer
God,
you reveal yourself to us
in deeds of creation, redemption, and sanctification.
You are not, though, what you do: you, simply, are.
Blessed the people you choose to enter into holy relationship with you.
You are love; envelop us into your mystery. Amen.

THE MOST HOLY BODY AND BLOOD OF CHRIST (CORPUS CHRISTI)

Gospel **(Mark 14:12-16, 22-26; L168B)**

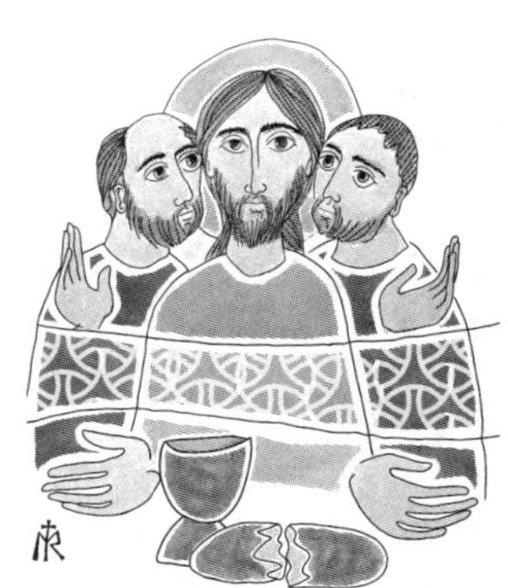

On the first day of the Feast of Unleavened Bread, when they sacrificed the Passover lamb, Jesus' disciples said to him, "Where do you want us to go and prepare for you to eat the Passover?" He sent two of his disciples and said to them, "Go into the city and a man will meet you, carrying a jar of water. Follow him. Wherever he enters, say to the master of the house, 'The Teacher says, "Where is my guest room where I may eat the Passover with my disciples?"' Then he will show you a large upper room furnished and ready. Make the preparations for us there." The disciples then went off, entered the city, and found it just as he had told them; and they prepared the Passover.

While they were eating, he took bread, said the blessing, broke it, gave it to them, and said, "Take it; this is my body." Then he took a cup, gave thanks, and gave it to them, and they all drank from it. He said to them, "This is my blood of the covenant, which will be shed for many. Amen, I say to you, I shall not drink again the fruit of the vine until the day when I drink it new in the kingdom of God." Then, after singing a hymn, they went out to the Mount of Olives.

First Reading **(Exod 24:3-8)**

When Moses came to the people and related all the words and ordinances of the LORD, they all answered with one voice, "We will do everything that the LORD has told us." Moses then wrote down all the words of the LORD and, rising early the next day, he erected at the foot of the mountain an altar and twelve pillars for the twelve tribes of Israel. Then, having sent certain young men of the Israelites to offer holocausts and sacrifice young bulls as peace offerings to the LORD, Moses took half of the blood and put it in large bowls; the other half he splashed on the altar. Taking the book of the covenant, he read it aloud to the people, who answered, "All that the LORD has said, we will heed and do." Then he took the blood and sprinkled it on the people, saying, "This is the blood of the covenant that the LORD has made with you in accordance with all these words of his."

***Responsorial Psalm* (Ps 116:12-13, 15-16, 17-18)**

℟. (13) I will take the cup of salvation, and call on the name of the Lord.
or: ℟. Alleluia.

How shall I make a return to the LORD
for all the good he has done for me?
The cup of salvation I will take up,
and I will call upon the name of the LORD.

℟. I will take the cup of salvation, and call on the name of the Lord.
or: ℟. Alleluia.

Precious in the eyes of the LORD
is the death of his faithful ones.
I am your servant, the son of your handmaid;
you have loosed my bonds.

℟. I will take the cup of salvation, and call on the name of the Lord.
or: ℟. Alleluia.

To you will I offer sacrifice of thanksgiving,
and I will call upon the name of the LORD.
My vows to the LORD I will pay
in the presence of all his people.

℟. I will take the cup of salvation, and call on the name of the Lord.
or: ℟. Alleluia.

See Appendix, p. 207, for Second Reading

Reflecting on Living the Gospel

Jesus's words over the bread and wine, then sharing it with his disciples, signifies his giving them a share in the atoning power of his death. And that atoning power has as its goal eternal life with Jesus. But it was not just those who sat at the table with Jesus who are able to share in the atoning power of Jesus's sacrifice; Jesus opened the way for all to share in the "eternal inheritance" (second reading). So walk with joy to share a foretaste of the unending banquet.

THE MOST HOLY BODY AND BLOOD OF CHRIST (CORPUS CHRISTI)

Connecting the Responsorial Psalm to the Readings

In the first verse of today's psalm, the psalmist asks, "How shall I make a return to the Lord / for all the good he has done for me?" While this line might spur us to consider a multitude of "goods" we have received from God, the original author sought to particularly thank God for his help when "I was caught by the bonds of death" (Ps 116:3; NABRE). Now that these bonds are "loosed," the faithful one seeks to "offer sacrifice of thanksgiving" in appreciation and recognition of God's care and healing power. Today we celebrate the feast of the Most Holy Body and Blood of Christ. Our "cup of salvation" is the chalice that holds the precious blood of Jesus. In his apostolic exhortation The Joy of the Gospel, Pope Francis urges us to consider the Eucharist, "not as a prize for the perfect but a powerful medicine and nourishment for the weak" (47). As the second reading assures us, "[I]f the blood of goats and bulls / and the sprinkling of a heifer's ashes / can sanctify those who are defiled / so that their flesh is cleansed, / how much more will the blood of Christ . . . cleanse our consciences from dead works / to worship the living God."

Psalmist Preparation

How do you experience the Eucharist as a sacrament of healing? Where are you most in need of healing at this moment in your life?

Prayer

God of the living,
you are the bread that sustains us, you are *the cup of salvation.*
You are body, blood, soul, and divinity,
so much more than our senses understand,
so simply understood: sacrificial love, and strength for the journey.
Hear our gratitude and praise. Amen.

JUNE 13, 2021

***Gospel* (Mark 4:26-34; L92B)**

Jesus said to the crowds: "This is how it is with the kingdom of God; it is as if a man were to scatter seed on the land and would sleep and rise night and day and through it all the seed would sprout and grow, he knows not how. Of its own accord the land yields fruit, first the blade, then the ear, then the full grain in the ear. And when the grain is ripe, he wields the sickle at once, for the harvest has come."

He said, "To what shall we compare the kingdom of God, or what parable can we use for it? It is like a mustard seed that, when it is sown in the ground, is the smallest of all the seeds on the earth. But once it is sown, it springs up and becomes the largest of plants and puts forth large branches, so that the birds of the sky can dwell in its shade." With many such parables he spoke the word to them as they were able to understand it. Without parables he did not speak to them, but to his own disciples he explained everything in private.

***First Reading* (Ezek 17:22-24)**

Thus says the Lord GOD:

I, too, will take from the crest of the cedar,
 from its topmost branches tear off a tender shoot,
and plant it on a high and lofty mountain;
 on the mountain heights of Israel I will plant it.
It shall put forth branches and bear fruit,
 and become a majestic cedar.
Birds of every kind shall dwell beneath it,
 every winged thing in the shade of its boughs.
And all the trees of the field shall know
 that I, the LORD,
bring low the high tree,
 lift high the lowly tree,
wither up the green tree,
 and make the withered tree bloom.
As I, the LORD, have spoken, so will I do.

ELEVENTH SUNDAY IN ORDINARY TIME

Responsorial Psalm **(Ps 92:2-3, 13-14, 15-16)**

℟. (cf. 2a) Lord, it is good to give thanks to you.

It is good to give thanks to the LORD,
to sing praise to your name, Most High,
to proclaim your kindness at dawn
and your faithfulness throughout the night.

℟. Lord, it is good to give thanks to you.

The just one shall flourish like the palm tree,
like a cedar of Lebanon shall he grow.
They that are planted in the house of the LORD
shall flourish in the courts of our God.

℟. Lord, it is good to give thanks to you.

They shall bear fruit even in old age;
vigorous and sturdy shall they be,
declaring how just is the LORD,
my rock, in whom there is no wrong.

℟. Lord, it is good to give thanks to you.

Second Reading **(2 Cor 5:6-10)**

Reflecting on Living the Gospel

The parable of the mustard seed is one of encouragement for struggling communities frustrated or despondent because of what seems the small and insignificant growth of the kingdom of God and its impact on the world. The mustard bush does not exist only for itself, but it offers a welcoming refuge for birds that nest in its shade. So the Christian community should spread out its branches in welcome to others, especially to those who are enduring the heat of suffering or searching either physically or spiritually for some "shade."

Connecting the Responsorial Psalm to the Readings

Our responsorial psalm reminds us of the foundation for all prayer: offering thanksgiving to God. Only with eyes of gratitude can we perceive the action of the Lord in our lives from "dawn" to dusk and all "throughout the night." As in the first reading and in the gospel, today's psalm also speaks of plants flourishing, this time palms and cedars, "planted in the house of the Lord." The gospel reminds us of a farmer who scatters seeds on the ground and then waits for them to "sprout and grow, / he knows not how." The farmer trusts that within the depths of the ground the seed is sending down roots that will eventually produce fruit he can see and harvest.

Psalmist Preparation

At times it is difficult to witness the action of God's grace within ourselves and others, but today's psalm encourages us that if we are "planted in the house of the Lord," we will flourish and grow. How do you experience your time of prayer and worship in "the house of the Lord" as the soil in which your own faith is planted?

Prayer

Generous God,
you are bountiful goodness and overflowing charity.
You know our every need before even we do ourselves.
It is good to give thanks to you.
You have no need of our praise;
that we can lift our voices to you is yet another divine gift.
Thank you. Amen.

TWELFTH SUNDAY IN ORDINARY TIME

***Gospel* (Mark 4:35-41; L95B)**

On that day, as evening drew on, Jesus said to his disciples: "Let us cross to the other side." Leaving the crowd, they took Jesus with them in the boat just as he was. And other boats were with him. A violent squall came up and waves were breaking over the boat, so that it was already filling up. Jesus was in the stern, asleep on a cushion. They woke him and said to him, "Teacher, do you not care that we are perishing?" He woke up, rebuked the wind, and said to the sea, "Quiet! Be still!" The wind ceased and there was great calm. Then he asked them, "Why are you terrified? Do you not yet have faith?" They were filled with great awe and said to one another, "Who then is this whom even wind and sea obey?"

***First Reading* (Job 38:1, 8-11)**

The Lord addressed Job out of the storm and said:
Who shut within doors the sea,
  when it burst forth from the womb;
when I made the clouds its garment
  and thick darkness its swaddling bands?
When I set limits for it
  and fastened the bar of its door,
and said: Thus far shall you come but no farther,
  and here shall your proud waves be stilled!

***Responsorial Psalm* (Ps 107:23-24, 25-26, 28-29, 30-31)**

℟. (1b) Give thanks to the Lord, his love is everlasting.
or: ℟. Alleluia.

They who sailed the sea in ships,
  trading on the deep waters,
these saw the works of the LORD
  and his wonders in the abyss.

℟. Give thanks to the Lord, his love is everlasting.
or: ℟. Alleluia.

His command raised up a storm wind
which tossed its waves on high.
They mounted up to heaven; they sank to the depths;
their hearts melted away in their plight.

℟. Give thanks to the Lord, his love is everlasting.
or: ℟. Alleluia.

They cried to the LORD in their distress;
from their straits he rescued them,
he hushed the storm to a gentle breeze,
and the billows of the sea were stilled.

℟. Give thanks to the Lord, his love is everlasting.
or: ℟. Alleluia.

They rejoiced that they were calmed,
and he brought them to their desired haven.
Let them give thanks to the LORD for his kindness
and his wondrous deeds to the children of men.

℟. Give thanks to the Lord, his love is everlasting.
or: ℟. Alleluia.

Second Reading **(2 Cor 5:14-17)**

Reflecting on Living the Gospel

The Jesus who has risen from the sleep of death is the faithful hope of every disciple. Often storms sweep down on us as suddenly as the wind and waves on the Sea of Galilee, and we find ourselves unprepared for sickness, a terminal diagnosis for ourselves or a loved one, difficult personal relations, job loss. We may find ourselves saying: "Teacher, do you not care that we are perishing?" Yet Jesus is present in the storms and will bring us to the shore of new beginnings and new initiatives.

Connecting the Responsorial Psalm to the Readings

Today's responsorial psalm reminds us of the reason for our hope, the everlasting love of God. In the gospel we see Jesus acting out the words of the psalmist as he "hush[es] the storm to a gentle breeze" and calms "the billows of the sea."

TWELFTH SUNDAY IN ORDINARY TIME

Psalmist Preparation

How do you experience God's compassion, protection, and guidance in the midst of life's storms?

Prayer

Triune God,
your *love is everlasting;*
you are a community of love, and bid us to be one as well.
Help us so to love our neighbors and indeed to love ourselves,
for you take up residence within each human person,
a temple of the Holy Spirit. Amen.

THIRTEENTH SUNDAY IN ORDINARY TIME

JUNE 27, 2021

***Gospel* (Mark 5:21-43 [or 5:21-24, 35b-43]; L98B)**

When Jesus had crossed again in the boat to the other side, a large crowd gathered around him, and he stayed close to the sea. One of the synagogue officials, named Jairus, came forward. Seeing him he fell at his feet and pleaded earnestly with him, saying, "My daughter is at the point of death. Please, come lay your hands on her that she may get well and live." He went off with him, and a large crowd followed him and pressed upon him.

There was a woman afflicted with hemorrhages for twelve years. She had suffered greatly at the hands of many doctors and had spent all that she had. Yet she was not helped but only grew worse. She had heard about Jesus and came up behind him in the crowd and touched his cloak. She said, "If I but touch his clothes, I shall be cured." Immediately her flow of blood dried up. She felt in her body that she was healed of her affliction. Jesus, aware at once that power had gone out from him, turned around in the crowd and asked, "Who has touched my clothes?" But his disciples said to Jesus, "You see how the crowd is pressing upon you, and yet you ask, 'Who touched me?'" And he looked around to see who had done it. The woman, realizing what had happened to her, approached in fear and trembling. She fell down before Jesus and told him the whole truth. He said to her, "Daughter, your faith has saved you. Go in peace and be cured of your affliction."

While he was still speaking, people from the synagogue official's house arrived and said, "Your daughter has died; why trouble the teacher any longer?" Disregarding the message that was reported, Jesus said to the synagogue official, "Do not be afraid; just have faith." He did not allow anyone to accompany him inside except Peter, James, and John, the brother of James. When they arrived at the house of the synagogue official, he caught sight of a commotion, people weeping and wailing loudly. So he went in and said to them, "Why this commotion and weeping? The child is not dead but asleep." And they ridiculed him. Then he put them all out. He took along the child's father and mother and those who were with him and entered the room where the child was. He took the child by the hand and said to her, *"Talitha koum,"* which means, "Little girl, I say to you, arise!" The girl, a child of twelve, arose immediately and walked around. At that they were utterly astounded. He gave strict orders that no one should know this and said that she should be given something to eat.

***First Reading* (Wis 1:13-15; 2:23-24)**

God did not make death,
nor does he rejoice in the destruction of the living.
For he fashioned all things that they might have being;
and the creatures of the world are wholesome,
and there is not a destructive drug among them
nor any domain of the netherworld on earth,
for justice is undying.
For God formed man to be imperishable;
the image of his own nature he made him.
But by the envy of the devil, death entered the world,
and they who belong to his company experience it.

***Responsorial Psalm* (Ps 30:2, 4, 5-6, 11, 12, 13)**

℟. (2a) I will praise you, Lord, for you have rescued me.

I will extol you, O LORD, for you drew me clear
and did not let my enemies rejoice over me.
O LORD, you brought me up from the netherworld;
you preserved me from among those going down into the pit.

℟. I will praise you, Lord, for you have rescued me.

Sing praise to the LORD, you his faithful ones,
and give thanks to his holy name.
For his anger lasts but a moment;
a lifetime, his good will.
At nightfall, weeping enters in,
but with the dawn, rejoicing.

℟. I will praise you, Lord, for you have rescued me.

Hear, O LORD, and have pity on me;
O LORD, be my helper.
You changed my mourning into dancing;
O LORD, my God, forever will I give you thanks.

℟. I will praise you, Lord, for you have rescued me.

Second Reading (2 Cor 8:7, 9, 13-15)

Reflecting on Living the Gospel

Both women in today's gospel reading announce to us the situation of women throughout the world who, for whatever reason, are still conditioned or condemned to insignificance or abuse; all those women who are still marginalized by society, yet who grasp bravely at other possibilities. Nor can the church opt out of its responsibility. The church's teaching about nondiscrimination needs to be applied to its own affairs. It must refer constantly back to Jesus and his way of relating to women and men in the Scriptures.

Connecting the Responsorial Psalm to the Readings

In its entirety, Psalm 30 is a hymn of praise whose author has been saved from a life-threatening illness. The psalmist writes in the third verse, "O LORD, my God, / I cried out to you for help and you healed me" (30:3; NABRE). For this reason the psalmist praises God, exulting, "You changed my mourning into dancing." In today's gospel, when Jesus arrives at Jairus's house, "weeping and wailing" for Jairus's daughter has already begun. After Jesus heals the girl, the onlookers "were utterly astounded." We can only imagine the rejoicing that must have taken place after having a beloved child restored to life and health.

Psalmist Preparation

Throughout life we encounter moments of joy and moments of deep suffering and grief. As you prepare to proclaim Psalm 30, consider how you have experienced God's healing and life-giving presence even when overcome by sorrow. In the midst of life's difficulties, how do you continue to proclaim the goodness of God?

Prayer

Abba God,
even within the greater community of faith,
increase my faith, deepen my relationship with you.
In times of darkness and distress, *you have rescued me.*
May I ever praise you, and extol your name in the midst of your
holy people,
you who live and reign forever and ever. Amen.

FOURTEENTH SUNDAY IN ORDINARY TIME

***Gospel* (Mark 6:1-6; L101B)**

Jesus departed from there and came to his native place, accompanied by his disciples. When the sabbath came he began to teach in the synagogue, and many who heard him were astonished. They said, "Where did this man get all this? What kind of wisdom has been given him? What mighty deeds are wrought by his hands! Is he not the carpenter, the son of Mary, and the brother of James and Joses and Judas and Simon? And are not his sisters here with us?" And they took offense at him. Jesus said to them, "A prophet is not without honor except in his native place and among his own kin and in his own house." So he was not able to perform any mighty deed there, apart from curing a few sick people by laying his hands on them. He was amazed at their lack of faith.

***First Reading* (Ezek 2:2-5)**

As the LORD spoke to me, the spirit entered into me and set me on my feet, and I heard the one who was speaking say to me: Son of man, I am sending you to the Israelites, rebels who have rebelled against me; they and their ancestors have revolted against me to this very day. Hard of face and obstinate of heart are they to whom I am sending you. But you shall say to them: Thus says the Lord GOD! And whether they heed or resist—for they are a rebellious house—they shall know that a prophet has been among them.

***Responsorial Psalm* (Ps 123:1-2, 2, 3-4)**

℟. (2cd) Our eyes are fixed on the Lord, pleading for his mercy.

To you I lift up my eyes
who are enthroned in heaven—
As the eyes of servants
are on the hands of their masters.

℟. Our eyes are fixed on the Lord, pleading for his mercy.

As the eyes of a maid
  are on the hands of her mistress,
So are our eyes on the LORD, our God,
  till he have pity on us.

℟. Our eyes are fixed on the Lord, pleading for his mercy.

Have pity on us, O LORD, have pity on us,
  for we are more than sated with contempt;
our souls are more than sated
  with the mockery of the arrogant,
  with the contempt of the proud.

℟. Our eyes are fixed on the Lord, pleading for his mercy.

Second Reading (2 Cor 12:7-10)

Reflecting on Living the Gospel

Each reading this Sunday is about those who were singed by failure and vulnerability, but who continue to be a guiding light to their communities. That the "Word was made failure and died among us" is the source of our hope, not despair. We may still be more inclined to listen to those who appear to be prophets on the celebrity circuit rather than those with whom we rub shoulders daily. We need humble ongoing and gospel-based discernment of the authenticity of prophets. Continued success is a dangerous criterion.

Connecting the Responsorial Psalm to the Readings

For the times we have failed to answer the call of God and have instead been "[h]ard of face and obstinate of heart," our psalm offers a prayer of repentance: "Our eyes are fixed on the Lord, pleading for his mercy." In our baptism we have each been called to take up the mantle of "priest, prophet, and king." To be a prophet in the footsteps of Ezekiel and following the way of Christ, we must first listen before we speak. With eyes fixed upon the Lord, we become oriented to God's fidelity, beauty, and truth. As our being is permeated with the word and the presence of the Lord, we are able to prophesy to God's goodness in all that we do and say.

FOURTEENTH SUNDAY IN ORDINARY TIME

Psalmist Preparation

This coming week, how might you rededicate yourself to fixing your eyes on the Lord?

Prayer

Immanent and transcendent God,
grant us your understanding, your perceptive heart and mind,
so that, while *our eyes are fixed on* you,
we may also see the hearts and minds of all those you have created and given dignity.
It is you who created all,
and you who imbue your creations with holiness. Amen.

JULY 11, 2021

Gospel (Mark 6:7-13; L104B)

Jesus summoned the Twelve and began to send them out two by two and gave them authority over unclean spirits. He instructed them to take nothing for the journey but a walking stick—no food, no sack, no money in their belts. They were, however, to wear sandals but not a second tunic. He said to them, "Wherever you enter a house, stay there until you leave. Whatever place does not welcome you or listen to you, leave there and shake the dust off your feet in testimony against them." So they went off and preached repentance. The Twelve drove out many demons, and they anointed with oil many who were sick and cured them.

First Reading (Amos 7:12-15)

Amaziah, priest of Bethel, said to Amos, "Off with you, visionary, flee to the land of Judah! There earn your bread by prophesying, but never again prophesy in Bethel; for it is the king's sanctuary and a royal temple." Amos answered Amaziah, "I was no prophet, nor have I belonged to a company of prophets; I was a shepherd and a dresser of sycamores. The LORD took me from following the flock, and said to me, Go, prophesy to my people Israel."

Responsorial Psalm (Ps 85:9-10, 11-12, 13-14)

℟. (8) Lord, let us see your kindness, and grant us your salvation.

I will hear what God proclaims;
 the LORD—for he proclaims peace.
Near indeed is his salvation to those who fear him,
 glory dwelling in our land.

℟. Lord, let us see your kindness, and grant us your salvation.

Kindness and truth shall meet;
 justice and peace shall kiss.
Truth shall spring out of the earth,
 and justice shall look down from heaven.

℟. Lord, let us see your kindness, and grant us your salvation.

FIFTEENTH SUNDAY IN ORDINARY TIME

The LORD himself will give his benefits;
our land shall yield its increase.
Justice shall walk before him,
and prepare the way of his steps.

℟. Lord, let us see your kindness, and grant us your salvation.

***Second Reading* (Eph 1:3-14 or 1:3-10)**

Reflecting on Living the Gospel

If they are not well received, the disciples are to leave, not with harsh words, but merely shaking off from their feet the dust of the unwelcoming place. We all need to "take upon's the mystery of things, / As if we were God's spies," said Shakespeare's King Lear. In the Christian sense, we are to be "God's spies," reconnoitering the possibilities for announcing the reigning presence of God in human lives in our own situations. And we must be prepared to fail, as Jesus and his followers failed.

Connecting the Responsorial Psalm to the Readings

In the first verse of today's psalm, the psalmist assures us, "I will hear what God proclaims / the Lord—for he proclaims peace." In the gospel and the first reading, Amos and the Twelve have listened deeply to God's word and now it is time for them to proclaim it to others.

Psalmist Preparation

We encounter God's proclamation of peace in many ways: reading the Bible, opening our hearts to God in prayer, and listening to the prophetic voices of others. How do you listen deeply for the voice of God in your life?

Prayer

God of the prophets,
many times it is easier for us to shun those who speak your truth.
We turn our backs on your voice;
you continually call us to conversion.
In these times, great redeemer,
let us see your kindness, and grant us your salvation. Amen.

SIXTEENTH SUNDAY IN ORDINARY TIME

JULY 18, 2021

***Gospel* (Mark 6:30-34; L107B)**

The apostles gathered together with Jesus and reported all they had done and taught. He said to them, "Come away by yourselves to a deserted place and rest a while." People were coming and going in great numbers, and they had no opportunity even to eat. So they went off in the boat by themselves to a deserted place. People saw them leaving and many came to know about it. They hastened there on foot from all the towns and arrived at the place before them.

When he disembarked and saw the vast crowd, his heart was moved with pity for them, for they were like sheep without a shepherd; and he began to teach them many things.

***First Reading* (Jer 23:1-6)**

Woe to the shepherds who mislead and scatter the flock of my pasture, says the LORD. Therefore, thus says the LORD, the God of Israel, against the shepherds who shepherd my people: You have scattered my sheep and driven them away. You have not cared for them, but I will take care to punish your evil deeds. I myself will gather the remnant of my flock from all the lands to which I have driven them and bring them back to their meadow; there they shall increase and multiply. I will appoint shepherds for them who will shepherd them so that they need no longer fear and tremble; and none shall be missing, says the LORD.

Behold, the days are coming, says the LORD,
  when I will raise up a righteous shoot to David;
as king he shall reign and govern wisely,
  he shall do what is just and right in the land.
In his days Judah shall be saved,
  Israel shall dwell in security.
This is the name they give him:
  "The LORD our justice."

SIXTEENTH SUNDAY IN ORDINARY TIME

***Responsorial Psalm* (Ps 23:1-3, 3-4, 5, 6)**

℟. (1) The Lord is my shepherd; there is nothing I shall want.

The LORD is my shepherd; I shall not want.
In verdant pastures he gives me repose;
beside restful waters he leads me;
he refreshes my soul.

℟. The Lord is my shepherd; there is nothing I shall want.

He guides me in right paths
for his name's sake.
Even though I walk in the dark valley
I fear no evil; for you are at my side
with your rod and your staff
that give me courage.

℟. The Lord is my shepherd; there is nothing I shall want.

You spread the table before me
in the sight of my foes;
you anoint my head with oil;
my cup overflows.

℟. The Lord is my shepherd; there is nothing I shall want.

Only goodness and kindness follow me
all the days of my life;
and I shall dwell in the house of the LORD
for years to come.

℟. The Lord is my shepherd; there is nothing I shall want.

***Second Reading* (Eph 2:13-18)**

Reflecting on Living the Gospel
Jesus gives us the priorities of the Good Shepherd: serve the people; care for the people; build up the people. These must be the priorities also of those called to shepherd the people today. All of us stumble, but true shepherds do not repeatedly put the sheep, especially the little ones, in harm's way, and then claim to be doing the work of the Lord. The Good Shepherd gave himself up for the sheep; woe to those shepherds who give up the sheep to protect themselves.

Connecting the Responsorial Psalm to the Readings

Today's psalm is attributed to David, the great king of Israel, who is "tending the sheep" (1 Sam 16:11) when we are first introduced to him in the Bible. This psalm offers details about shepherding that only a shepherd would know. For the shepherd, the welfare of his sheep is a constant preoccupation. He is responsible for their rest and their activity, their nourishment, and their health. In today's gospel, Jesus intends to find a quiet place the apostles could "rest a while." But when he sees the crowds longing to be fed with his life-giving words, he cannot turn his back on them. And so, just as a good shepherd would, he sets about tending to their needs.

Psalmist Preparation

How do you experience God's love and care for you as that of a shepherd tending his sheep?

Prayer

Good Shepherd,
your providence is beyond what we can understand.
In prayers of gratitude, lead each of us to truly exclaim,
there is nothing I shall want.
You fulfill every earnest desire and every need we have.
In your house, in your generosity, we dwell, forevermore. Amen.

SEVENTEENTH SUNDAY IN ORDINARY TIME

Gospel (John 6:1-15; L110B)

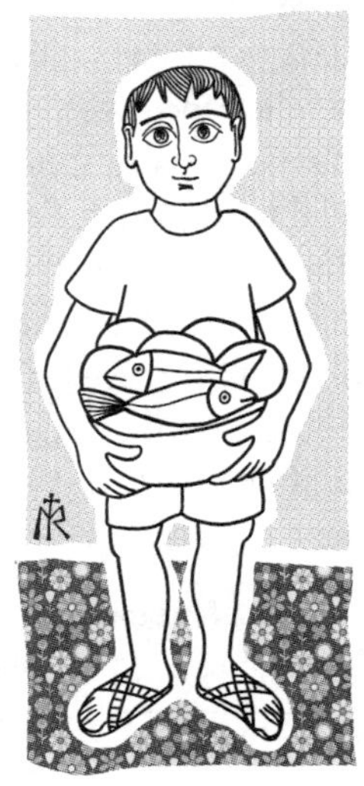

Jesus went across the Sea of Galilee. A large crowd followed him, because they saw the signs he was performing on the sick. Jesus went up on the mountain, and there he sat down with his disciples. The Jewish feast of Passover was near. When Jesus raised his eyes and saw that a large crowd was coming to him, he said to Philip, "Where can we buy enough food for them to eat?" He said this to test him, because he himself knew what he was going to do. Philip answered him, "Two hundred days' wages worth of food would not be enough for each of them to have a little." One of his disciples, Andrew, the brother of Simon Peter, said to him, "There is a boy here who has five barley loaves and two fish; but what good are these for so many?" Jesus said, "Have the people recline." Now there was a great deal of grass in that place. So the men reclined, about five thousand in number. Then Jesus took the loaves, gave thanks, and distributed them to those who were reclining, and also as much of the fish as they wanted. When they had had their fill, he said to his disciples, "Gather the fragments left over, so that nothing will be wasted." So they collected them, and filled twelve wicker baskets with fragments from the five barley loaves that had been more than they could eat. When the people saw the sign he had done, they said, "This is truly the Prophet, the one who is to come into the world." Since Jesus knew that they were going to come and carry him off to make him king, he withdrew again to the mountain alone.

First Reading (2 Kgs 4:42-44)

A man came from Baal-shalishah bringing to Elisha, the man of God, twenty barley loaves made from the firstfruits, and fresh grain in the ear. Elisha said, "Give it to the people to eat." But his servant objected, "How can I set this before a hundred people?" Elisha insisted, "Give it to the people to eat. For thus says the LORD, 'They shall eat and there shall be some left over.'" And when they had eaten, there was some left over, as the LORD had said.

***Responsorial Psalm* (Ps 145:10-11, 15-16, 17-18)**

℟. (cf. 16) The hand of the Lord feeds us; he answers all our needs.

Let all your works give you thanks, O LORD,
 and let your faithful ones bless you.
Let them discourse of the glory of your kingdom
 and speak of your might.

℟. The hand of the Lord feeds us; he answers all our needs.

The eyes of all look hopefully to you,
 and you give them their food in due season;
you open your hand
 and satisfy the desire of every living thing.

℟. The hand of the Lord feeds us; he answers all our needs.

The LORD is just in all his ways
 and holy in all his works.
The LORD is near to all who call upon him,
 to all who call upon him in truth.

℟. The hand of the Lord feeds us; he answers all our needs.

***Second Reading* (Eph 4:1-6)**

Reflecting on Living the Gospel

We bring to the Eucharist the little that we have, all the fragments of our inadequacies, our successes and failures, our hopes and fears. We offer them to God with the fruits of the earth and the work of human hands, and these small gifts are transformed and offered back to us as the gift of Jesus's sacramental Body and Blood, into whose life we are gathered. This is not logic, pragmatism, or self-satisfaction; this is *eucharistía*, thanksgiving for God's abundant and eternal generosity.

Connecting the Responsorial Psalm to the Readings

Today's responsorial psalm invites us to trust in the abundance and tenderness of God. This is not just a global or impersonal generosity, but the intimacy of a parent who feeds a child or a caregiver nurturing one who is ill or weak. We are fed by "the hand of the Lord," and in him alone "all our needs" are answered. In today's gospel, Jesus's hands grasp the barley loaves to bless them and distribute them to the hungry crowd.

SEVENTEENTH SUNDAY IN ORDINARY TIME

Psalmist Preparation

Over the next few weeks we will delve deeply into Jesus's discourse about the bread of life. As you prepare to encounter Jesus in the Eucharist, how do you experience the sacrament as being hand-fed by the Lord of all?

Prayer

Sustenance of all,
you bid us to be your hands and feet on earth.
When we struggle to discern this calling,
remind us that *the hand of the Lord feeds us; he answers all our needs.*
To be your body is to do these things,
in your name, for one another. Amen.

EIGHTEENTH SUNDAY IN ORDINARY TIME

AUGUST 1, 2021

Gospel **(John 6:24-35; L113B)**

When the crowd saw that neither Jesus nor his disciples were there, they themselves got into boats and came to Capernaum looking for Jesus. And when they found him across the sea they said to him, "Rabbi, when did you get here?" Jesus answered them and said, "Amen, amen, I say to you, you are looking for me not because you saw signs but because you ate the loaves and were filled. Do not work for food that perishes but for the food that endures for eternal life, which the Son of Man will give you. For on him the Father, God, has set his seal." So they said to him, "What can we do to accomplish the works of God?" Jesus answered and said to them, "This is the work of God, that you believe in the one he sent." So they said to him, "What sign can you do, that we may see and believe in you? What can you do? Our ancestors ate manna in the desert, as it is written:

He gave them bread from heaven to eat."

So Jesus said to them, "Amen, amen, I say to you, it was not Moses who gave the bread from heaven; my Father gives you the true bread from heaven. For the bread of God is that which comes down from heaven and gives life to the world."

So they said to him, "Sir, give us this bread always." Jesus said to them, "I am the bread of life; whoever comes to me will never hunger, and whoever believes in me will never thirst."

First Reading **(Exod 16:2-4, 12-15)**

The whole Israelite community grumbled against Moses and Aaron. The Israelites said to them, "Would that we had died at the LORD's hand in the land of Egypt, as we sat by our fleshpots and ate our fill of bread! But you had to lead us into this desert to make the whole community die of famine!"

Then the LORD said to Moses, "I will now rain down bread from heaven for you. Each day the people are to go out and gather their daily portion; thus will I test them, to see whether they follow my instructions or not.

"I have heard the grumbling of the Israelites. Tell them: In the evening twilight you shall eat flesh, and in the morning you shall have your fill of bread, so that you may know that I, the LORD, am your God."

In the evening quail came up and covered the camp. In the morning a dew lay all about the camp, and when the dew evaporated, there on the surface of the desert were fine flakes like hoarfrost on the ground. On seeing it, the Israelites asked one another, "What is this?" for they did not know what it was. But Moses told them, "This is the bread that the LORD has given you to eat."

Responsorial Psalm **(Ps 78:3-4, 23-24, 25, 54)**

℟. (24b) The Lord gave them bread from heaven.

What we have heard and know,
and what our fathers have declared to us,
we will declare to the generation to come
the glorious deeds of the LORD and his strength
and the wonders that he wrought.

℟. The Lord gave them bread from heaven.

He commanded the skies above
and opened the doors of heaven;
he rained manna upon them for food
and gave them heavenly bread.

℟. The Lord gave them bread from heaven.

Man ate the bread of angels,
food he sent them in abundance.
And he brought them to his holy land,
to the mountains his right hand had won.

℟. The Lord gave them bread from heaven.

Second Reading **(Eph 4:17, 20-24)**

Reflecting on Living the Gospel

In the Jewish tradition the manna in the desert was associated with the giving of the Torah, and the wisdom of God is often portrayed by the metaphor of food. While speaking of the bread of life, Jesus uses language of believing, drawing near, and listening, terms associated more with assimilation of wisdom than eating. Full participation in eating the body and drinking the blood of Jesus follows upon personal commitment and love which draws a person to absorb the teaching of Jesus and imitate his life given for others.

Connecting the Responsorial Psalm to the Readings

Today's psalm recalls the gift of manna in the desert by proclaiming, "The Lord gave them bread from heaven." It is a psalm of faith and hope with the people responding to God's saving acts by promising to "declare to the generation to come / the glorious deeds of the Lord and his strength / and the wonders that he has wrought." As Christians, we also find in today's psalm a reference to Christ, the Bread of Life, who continues to be our heavenly food at the eucharistic banquet.

Psalmist Preparation

What are the glorious deeds and wonders the Lord has wrought in your life and how do you proclaim his faithfulness and love to those you meet?

Prayer

God of Providence,
you sustain us not by bread alone,
but by every word that comes forth from your mouth.
Still you feed our bodies today as you always have:
first, manna as food for the journey, and now by the *bread from heaven*,
your son, Christ, our Lord. Amen.

NINETEENTH SUNDAY IN ORDINARY TIME

***Gospel* (John 6:41-51; L116B)**

The Jews murmured about Jesus because he said, "I am the bread that came down from heaven," and they said, "Is this not Jesus, the son of Joseph? Do we not know his father and mother? Then how can he say, 'I have come down from heaven'?" Jesus answered and said to them, "Stop murmuring among yourselves. No one can come to me unless the Father who sent me draw him, and I will raise him on the last day. It is written in the prophets:

They shall all be taught by God.

Everyone who listens to my Father and learns from him comes to me. Not that anyone has seen the Father except the one who is from God; he has seen the Father. Amen, amen, I say to you, whoever believes has eternal life. I am the bread of life. Your ancestors ate the manna in the desert, but they died; this is the bread that comes down from heaven so that one may eat it and not die. I am the living bread that came down from heaven; whoever eats this bread will live forever; and the bread that I will give is my flesh for the life of the world."

***First Reading* (1 Kgs 19:4-8)**

Elijah went a day's journey into the desert, until he came to a broom tree and sat beneath it. He prayed for death, saying: "This is enough, O LORD! Take my life, for I am no better than my fathers." He lay down and fell asleep under the broom tree, but then an angel touched him and ordered him to get up and eat. Elijah looked and there at his head was a hearth cake and a jug of water. After he ate and drank, he lay down again, but the angel of the LORD came back a second time, touched him, and ordered, "Get up and eat, else the journey will be too long for you!" He got up, ate, and drank; then strengthened by that food, he walked forty days and forty nights to the mountain of God, Horeb.

Responsorial Psalm **(Ps 34:2-3, 4-5, 6-7, 8-9)**

℟. (9a) Taste and see the goodness of the Lord.

I will bless the LORD at all times;
 his praise shall be ever in my mouth.
Let my soul glory in the LORD;
 the lowly will hear me and be glad.

℟. Taste and see the goodness of the Lord.

Glorify the LORD with me,
 let us together extol his name.
I sought the LORD, and he answered me
 and delivered me from all my fears.

℟. Taste and see the goodness of the Lord.

Look to him that you may be radiant with joy,
 and your faces may not blush with shame.
When the afflicted man called out, the LORD heard,
 and from all his distress he saved him.

℟. Taste and see the goodness of the Lord.

The angel of the LORD encamps
 around those who fear him and delivers them.
Taste and see how good the LORD is;
 blessed the man who takes refuge in him.

℟. Taste and see the goodness of the Lord.

Second Reading **(Eph 4:30–5:2)**

Reflecting on Living the Gospel

In the continuation of the reading from John 6 there is movement to another level of understanding of what Jesus means by "bread": from material bread, to the bread that is the work of faith, and now to the bread that is Jesus himself. We should not be too eager to hurry on to eucharistic references—not yet. The challenge is to recognize Jesus as the revelation of God's word. When people come to him, his words become a source of life.

NINETEENTH SUNDAY IN ORDINARY TIME

Connecting the Responsorial Psalm to the Readings

This is our second Sunday reading from the bread of life discourse in John's gospel and considering the Eucharist as the food that sustains and nurtures us for eternal life. Today's responsorial psalm invites us to "[t]aste and see the goodness of the Lord." Our God wants us to know him with all our senses. It was not enough for God to reveal himself to us through creation or even in the human body of Jesus Christ. Throughout the ages, the resurrected Lord is made present to us in a way that we both taste and see as the Eucharist, the Bread that is Jesus's "flesh for the life of the world." For this reason, we "bless the Lord at all times."

Psalmist Preparation

Consider the gift of the Eucharist in your life. When did you first receive this sacrament and how has your relationship with the Lord grown over the years of being invited to feast at the Lord's table?

Prayer

Good and gracious God,
there are times it is difficult to perceive your presence in our lives.
Help us to recognize,
in times of clamor, discord, struggle, confusion, and despair,
your eternal offering to us: to *taste and see* your goodness,
and welcome you into our very beings. Amen.

THE ASSUMPTION OF THE BLESSED VIRGIN MARY

AUGUST 15, 2021

***Gospel* (Luke 1:39-56; L622)**

Mary set out and traveled to the hill country in haste to a town of Judah, where she entered the house of Zechariah and greeted Elizabeth. When Elizabeth heard Mary's greeting, the infant leaped in her womb, and Elizabeth, filled with the Holy Spirit, cried out in a loud voice and said, "Blessed are you among women, and blessed is the fruit of your womb. And how does this happen to me, that the mother of my Lord should come to me? For at the moment the sound of your greeting reached my ears, the infant in my womb leaped for joy. Blessed are you who believed that what was spoken to you by the Lord would be fulfilled."

And Mary said:

"My soul proclaims the greatness of the Lord;
  my spirit rejoices in God my Savior
  for he has looked with favor upon his lowly servant.
From this day all generations will call me blessed:
  the Almighty has done great things for me,
  and holy is his Name.
  He has mercy on those who fear him
  in every generation.
He has shown the strength of his arm,
  and has scattered the proud in their conceit.
He has cast down the mighty from their thrones,
  and has lifted up the lowly.
He has filled the hungry with good things,
  and the rich he has sent away empty.
He has come to the help of his servant Israel
  for he has remembered his promise of mercy,
  the promise he made to our fathers,
  to Abraham and his children forever."

Mary remained with her about three months and then returned to her home.

THE ASSUMPTION OF THE BLESSED VIRGIN MARY

First Reading **(Rev 11:19a; 12:1-6a, 10ab)**

God's temple in heaven was opened, and the ark of his covenant could be seen in the temple.

A great sign appeared in the sky, a woman clothed with the sun, with the moon beneath her feet, and on her head a crown of twelve stars. She was with child and wailed aloud in pain as she labored to give birth. Then another sign appeared in the sky; it was a huge red dragon, with seven heads and ten horns, and on its heads were seven diadems. Its tail swept away a third of the stars in the sky and hurled them down to the earth. Then the dragon stood before the woman about to give birth, to devour her child when she gave birth. She gave birth to a son, a male child, destined to rule all the nations with an iron rod. Her child was caught up to God and his throne. The woman herself fled into the desert where she had a place prepared by God.

Then I heard a loud voice in heaven say:
"Now have salvation and power come,
and the Kingdom of our God
and the authority of his Anointed One."

Responsorial Psalm **(Ps 45:10, 11, 12, 16)**

℟. (10bc) The queen stands at your right hand, arrayed in gold.

The queen takes her place at your right hand in gold of Ophir.

℟. The queen stands at your right hand, arrayed in gold.

Hear, O daughter, and see; turn your ear,
forget your people and your father's house.

℟. The queen stands at your right hand, arrayed in gold.

So shall the king desire your beauty;
for he is your lord.

℟. The queen stands at your right hand, arrayed in gold.

They are borne in with gladness and joy;
they enter the palace of the king.

℟. The queen stands at your right hand, arrayed in gold.

See Appendix, p. 208, for Second Reading

Reflecting on Living the Gospel

The point of the Assumption is that Mary is in heaven with her Lord; she is not simply the stuff of myth or symbol. She was an actual flesh and blood woman, chosen above all people to play the most significant human role in the divine salvific plan. We should never lose track of her humanity. There is this temptation to dehumanize her, but this pays no justice to her faithfulness or to Mary as a model woman, someone women and men can follow as exemplary in trust and joy.

Connecting the Responsorial Psalm to the Readings

Today's psalm, which commemorates a royal wedding, is fitting for this day when we celebrate Mary, the Queen of Heaven, the Mother of God. The third verse describes the wedding guests who are "borne in with gladness and joy." We also encounter joy in the gospel when John the Baptist leaps within the womb of his mother, Elizabeth. John's joy signals the presence of Jesus, the one who is Emmanuel, God with us. We partake of this joy every time we draw near to the risen Lord in word and sacrament, or whenever his love is mediated to us through the compassion and service of another.

Psalmist Preparation

Today, how do you experience the joy of the Lord as you celebrate the feast of the Assumption?

Prayer

God,
you choose the small, weak, and voiceless
to bring your word to both disconsolate hearts and the proud of heart.
Your vessel, Mary, brought forth your Word
in flesh and bone, and was raised from lowly estate:
the queen stands at your right hand;
may we too one day know your eternal glory. Amen.

TWENTY-FIRST SUNDAY IN ORDINARY TIME

***Gospel* (John 6:60-69; L122B)**

Many of Jesus' disciples who were listening said, "This saying is hard; who can accept it?" Since Jesus knew that his disciples were murmuring about this, he said to them, "Does this shock you? What if you were to see the Son of Man ascending to where he was before? It is the spirit that gives life, while the flesh is of no avail. The words I have spoken to you are Spirit and life. But there are some of you who do not believe." Jesus knew from the beginning the ones who would not believe and the one who would betray him. And he said, "For this reason I have told you that no one can come to me unless it is granted him by my Father."

As a result of this, many of his disciples returned to their former way of life and no longer accompanied him. Jesus then said to the Twelve, "Do you also want to leave?" Simon Peter answered him, "Master, to whom shall we go? You have the words of eternal life. We have come to believe and are convinced that you are the Holy One of God."

***First Reading* (Josh 24:1-2a, 15-17, 18b)**

Joshua gathered together all the tribes of Israel at Shechem, summoning their elders, their leaders, their judges, and their officers. When they stood in ranks before God, Joshua addressed all the people: "If it does not please you to serve the LORD, decide today whom you will serve, the gods your fathers served beyond the River or the gods of the Amorites in whose country you are now dwelling. As for me and my household, we will serve the LORD."

But the people answered, "Far be it from us to forsake the LORD for the service of other gods. For it was the LORD, our God, who brought us and our fathers up out of the land of Egypt, out of a state of slavery. He performed those great miracles before our very eyes and protected us along our entire journey and among the peoples through whom we passed. Therefore we also will serve the LORD, for he is our God."

***Responsorial Psalm* (Ps 34:2-3, 16-17, 18-19, 20-21)**

℟. (9a) Taste and see the goodness of the Lord.

I will bless the LORD at all times;
his praise shall be ever in my mouth.
Let my soul glory in the LORD;
the lowly will hear me and be glad.

℟. Taste and see the goodness of the Lord.

The LORD has eyes for the just,
and ears for their cry.
The LORD confronts the evildoers,
to destroy remembrance of them from the earth.

℟. Taste and see the goodness of the Lord.

When the just cry out, the LORD hears them,
and from all their distress he rescues them.
The LORD is close to the brokenhearted;
and those who are crushed in spirit he saves.

℟. Taste and see the goodness of the Lord.

Many are the troubles of the just one,
but out of them all the LORD delivers him;
he watches over all his bones;
not one of them shall be broken.

℟. Taste and see the goodness of the Lord.

***Second Reading* (Eph 5:21-32 or 5:2a, 25-32)**

Reflecting on Living the Gospel

We are like the people listening to Jesus in this gospel: we can be tempted to want Jesus to conform to our expectations of how he should be present in and to his church in word and sacrament; we are intolerant of his willingness to be present in the poverty of so many eucharistic liturgies. But perhaps our greatest betrayal is our failure to realize that when we are not in communion with our sisters and brothers we fail to be in communion with the Body of Christ.

TWENTY-FIRST SUNDAY IN ORDINARY TIME

Connecting the Responsorial Psalm to the Readings

Today's psalm once again directs our attention to the Eucharist (as have the psalms from the Seventeenth, Eighteenth, and Nineteenth Sundays of Ordinary Time). In fact, today we return again to Psalm 34 with its beloved refrain, "Taste and see the goodness of the Lord." In our gospel, Jesus tells the crowd, "The words I have spoken to you are Spirit and life." Not only does Jesus wish to nourish us with his Body and Blood in the Eucharist, but also with the words of truth he speaks to all who would listen.

Psalmist Preparation

How does the word of God nourish and strengthen you in the life of faith?

Prayer

Holy and Blessed One,
sometimes it is hard to know you;
it is difficult to name one
who is so ineffable and incomprehensible.
Yet, *the goodness of the Lord*—your goodness—is ever-present,
and the most real and recognizable love we will ever know. Amen.

TWENTY-SECOND SUNDAY IN ORDINARY TIME

AUGUST 29, 2021

***Gospel* (Mark 7:1-8, 14-15, 21-23; L125B)**

When the Pharisees with some scribes who had come from Jerusalem gathered around Jesus, they observed that some of his disciples ate their meals with unclean, that is, unwashed, hands.—For the Pharisees and, in fact, all Jews, do not eat without carefully washing their hands, keeping the tradition of the elders. And on coming from the marketplace they do not eat without purifying themselves. And there are many other things that they have traditionally observed, the purification of cups and jugs and kettles and beds.—So the Pharisees and scribes questioned him, "Why do your disciples not follow the tradition of the elders but instead eat a meal with unclean hands?" He responded, "Well did Isaiah prophesy about you hypocrites, as it is written:

This people honors me with their lips,
but their hearts are far from me;
in vain do they worship me,
teaching as doctrines human precepts.

You disregard God's commandment but cling to human tradition."

He summoned the crowd again and said to them, "Hear me, all of you, and understand. Nothing that enters one from outside can defile that person; but the things that come out from within are what defile.

"From within people, from their hearts, come evil thoughts, unchastity, theft, murder, adultery, greed, malice, deceit, licentiousness, envy, blasphemy, arrogance, folly. All these evils come from within and they defile."

***First Reading* (Deut 4:1-2, 6-8)**

Moses said to the people: "Now, Israel, hear the statutes and decrees which I am teaching you to observe, that you may live, and may enter in and take possession of the land which the Lord, the God of your fathers, is giving you. In your observance of the commandments of the Lord, your God, which I enjoin upon you, you shall not add to what I command you nor subtract from it. Observe them carefully, for thus will you give evidence of your wisdom and intelligence to the nations, who will hear of all these statutes and say, 'This great nation is truly a wise and intelligent people.' For what great nation is there that has gods so close to it as the LORD, our God, is to us whenever we call upon him? Or what great nation has statutes and decrees that are as just as this whole law which I am setting before you today?"

***Responsorial Psalm* (Ps 15:2-3, 3-4, 4-5)**

℟. (1a) The one who does justice will live in the presence of the Lord.

Whoever walks blamelessly and does justice;
who thinks the truth in his heart
and slanders not with his tongue.

℟. The one who does justice will live in the presence of the Lord.

Who harms not his fellow man,
nor takes up a reproach against his neighbor;
by whom the reprobate is despised,
while he honors those who fear the LORD.

℟. The one who does justice will live in the presence of the Lord.

Who lends not his money at usury
and accepts no bribe against the innocent.
Whoever does these things
shall never be disturbed.

℟. The one who does justice will live in the presence of the Lord.

***Second Reading* (Jas 1:17-18, 21b-22, 27)**

Reflecting on Living the Gospel

Jesus responds to the Pharisees' challenge about the behavior of his disciples with a quotation from the prophet Isaiah, addressing them as "hypocrites." Out of the strong Jewish prophetic tradition of self-criticism, Isaiah spoke of religious practices that were on the lips but not in the heart as a superficial and external "playacting" at true religion. External rituals have value only insofar as they encourage or express the dedication of our hearts. Before we eat as a eucharistic community, are our hearts clean?

Connecting the Responsorial Psalm to the Readings

The spirit of the law is encapsulated in today's psalm. To follow the Lord is to "walk blamelessly and do justice," by embracing truth and charity in word and action. The first reading from Deuteronomy lauds the law as the bringer of wisdom and justice that also proves to the nations the closeness of God to the people of Israel. In today's gospel, Jesus reminds the Pharisees of the most important purpose of the law: to bring hearts close to God. While sin separates us from God and others, doing justice leads us to "live in the presence of the Lord."

Psalmist Preparation

How are you being called to live God's law with fidelity and courage?

Prayer

Universal God,
there is no peace like your peace, one of mercy and justice.
Teach us to live your ways and to be people of justice,
that we may always and ever *live in the presence of the Lord*,
your son, who lives and reigns forever and ever. Amen.

TWENTY-THIRD SUNDAY IN ORDINARY TIME

***Gospel* (Mark 7:31-37; L128B)**

Again Jesus left the district of Tyre and went by way of Sidon to the Sea of Galilee, into the district of the Decapolis. And people brought to him a deaf man who had a speech impediment and begged him to lay his hand on him. He took him off by himself away from the crowd. He put his finger into the man's ears and, spitting, touched his tongue; then he looked up to heaven and groaned, and said to him, *"Ephphatha!"*—that is, "Be opened!"—And immediately the man's ears were opened, his speech impediment was removed, and he spoke plainly. He ordered them not to tell anyone. But the more he ordered them not to, the more they proclaimed it. They were exceedingly astonished and they said, "He has done all things well. He makes the deaf hear and the mute speak."

***First Reading* (Isa 35:4-7a)**

Thus says the LORD:
Say to those whose hearts are frightened:
  Be strong, fear not!
Here is your God,
  he comes with vindication;
With divine recompense
  he comes to save you.
Then will the eyes of the blind be opened,
  the ears of the deaf be cleared;
Then will the lame leap like a stag,
  then the tongue of the mute will sing.
Streams will burst forth in the desert,
  and rivers in the steppe.
The burning sands will become pools,
  and the thirsty ground, springs of water.

***Responsorial Psalm* (Ps 146:6-7, 8-9a, 9bc-10)**

℟. (1b) Praise the Lord, my soul! *or:* ℟. Alleluia.

The God of Jacob keeps faith forever,
secures justice for the oppressed,
gives food to the hungry.
The LORD sets captives free.

℟. Praise the Lord, my soul! *or:* ℟. Alleluia.

The LORD gives sight to the blind;
the LORD raises up those who were bowed down.
The LORD loves the just;
the LORD protects strangers.

℟. Praise the Lord, my soul! *or:* ℟. Alleluia.

The fatherless and the widow the LORD sustains,
but the way of the wicked he thwarts.
The LORD shall reign forever;
your God, O Zion, through all generations. Alleluia.

℟. Praise the Lord, my soul! *or:* ℟. Alleluia.

***Second Reading* (Jas 2:1-5)**

Reflecting on Living the Gospel

To the man who is deaf and has an impediment in his speech, Jesus speaks a single word: "*Ephphatha!*" "Be opened!" The fact that Mark retained the Aramaic adds a note of respect for the human words of Jesus. It would not have been an unintelligible word or a magical incantation in the original context. It is important that all who come to Jesus recognize this as the command to be open to God's will, open to healing of the suffering of our brothers and sisters.

Connecting the Responsorial Psalm to the Readings

The triumphant nature of Psalm 146 calls us to praise and worship the Lord who "shall reign forever." Similar to the prophecy from Isaiah, within this psalm we are given insight into God's dreams for the world. God envisions and intends a social order where the hungry are filled, the captives freed, the blind see, the bowed down are raised, and the stranger, widow, and orphan are sustained. Not only are these comforting images to bring us consolation in times of grief and suffering, they are also a call to action. As the Body of Christ, we are meant to help bring about this kingdom where justice and mercy reign.

TWENTY-THIRD SUNDAY IN ORDINARY TIME

Psalmist Preparation

Today's psalm contains good news for the poor, the hungry, and the oppressed—and also a warning for the wicked whose ways God will "thwart." These Scripture passages that champion the vulnerable and weak of society invite us to discern where we stand on social issues. Are we in tune with the needs of the poorest of the poor or do we align ourselves with the powerful? This week, consider how today's psalm might call you to ongoing conversion as a disciple of Christ.

Prayer

God of Jacob and Leah,
show to each of us your faithfulness, heal our ills, feed us and set us free!
You are ever present and always love, in every land and age.
Praise the Lord, my soul, we exclaim.
Alleluia, we praise your name. Amen.

TWENTY-FOURTH SUNDAY IN ORDINARY TIME

SEPTEMBER 12, 2021

***Gospel* (Mark 8:27-35; L131B)**

Jesus and his disciples set out for the villages of Caesarea Philippi. Along the way he asked his disciples, "Who do people say that I am?" They said in reply, "John the Baptist, others Elijah, still others one of the prophets." And he asked them, "But who do you say that I am?" Peter said to him in reply, "You are the Christ." Then he warned them not to tell anyone about him.

He began to teach them that the Son of Man must suffer greatly and be rejected by the elders, the chief priests, and the scribes, and be killed, and rise after three days. He spoke this openly. Then Peter took him aside and began to rebuke him. At this he turned around and, looking at his disciples, rebuked Peter and said, "Get behind me, Satan. You are thinking not as God does, but as human beings do."

He summoned the crowd with his disciples and said to them, "Whoever wishes to come after me must deny himself, take up his cross, and follow me. For whoever wishes to save his life will lose it, but whoever loses his life for my sake and that of the gospel will save it."

***First Reading* (Isa 50:4c-9a)**

The Lord GOD opens my ear that I may hear;
and I have not rebelled,
have not turned back.
I gave my back to those who beat me,
my cheeks to those who plucked my beard;
My face I did not shield
from buffets and spitting.

The Lord GOD is my help,
therefore I am not disgraced;
I have set my face like flint,
knowing that I shall not be put to shame.
He is near who upholds my right;
if anyone wishes to oppose me,
let us appear together.

Who disputes my right?
   Let that man confront me.
See, the Lord GOD is my help;
   who will prove me wrong?

***Responsorial Psalm* (Ps 116:1-2, 3-4, 5-6, 8-9)**

℟. (9) I will walk before the Lord, in the land of the living.
or: ℟. Alleluia.

I love the LORD because he has heard
   my voice in supplication,
because he has inclined his ear to me
   the day I called.

℟. I will walk before the Lord, in the land of the living.
or: ℟. Alleluia.

The cords of death encompassed me;
   the snares of the netherworld seized upon me;
   I fell into distress and sorrow,
And I called upon the name of the LORD,
   "O LORD, save my life!"

℟. I will walk before the Lord, in the land of the living.
or: ℟. Alleluia.

Gracious is the LORD and just;
   yes, our God is merciful.
The LORD keeps the little ones;
   I was brought low, and he saved me.

℟. I will walk before the Lord, in the land of the living.
or: ℟. Alleluia.

For he has freed my soul from death,
   my eyes from tears, my feet from stumbling.
I shall walk before the LORD
   in the land of the living.

℟. I will walk before the Lord, in the land of the living.
or: ℟. Alleluia.

***Second Reading* (Jas 2:14-18)**

Reflecting on Living the Gospel

The Czech theologian Tomáš Halík says, "If we have never had the feeling that what Jesus wants of us is absurd, crazy, and impossible, then we've probably either been too hasty in taming or diluting the radical nature of his teaching with soothing intellectualizing interpretations, or have too easily forgotten to what extent our thinking, customs, and actions are rooted 'in this world.'" Jesus offers "God's thinking," the thinking by which we save our lives by losing them and build a kingdom whose divine power is seen as human weakness.

Connecting the Responsorial Psalm to the Readings

In today's gospel Jesus predicts not only his passion, but also his resurrection. Just as Peter does, when we read that "the Son of Man must suffer greatly / be rejected by the elders, the chief priests, and the scribes, / and be killed, and rise after three days," we might focus on the dark events of this narrative rather than the outcome. Death is not the end here. Today's responsorial psalm can be prayed as our own affirmation of life coming from death in the resurrection. No matter what events befall us we believe, "I will walk before the Lord, in the land of the living."

Psalmist Preparation

How does belief in the resurrection affect the way you live?

Prayer

Gracious God,
we yearn to know your presence, you dwell in your warmth and light.
On our pilgrimage of faith, we seek to journey with you, before you,
here, *in the land of the living.*
Free us from all that separates us from you,
who are Lord forever and ever. Amen.

TWENTY-FIFTH SUNDAY IN ORDINARY TIME

***Gospel* (Mark 9:30-37; L134B)**

Jesus and his disciples left from there and began a journey through Galilee, but he did not wish anyone to know about it. He was teaching his disciples and telling them, "The Son of Man is to be handed over to men and they will kill him, and three days after his death the Son of Man will rise." But they did not understand the saying, and they were afraid to question him.

They came to Capernaum and, once inside the house, he began to ask them, "What were you arguing about on the way?" But they remained silent. They had been discussing among themselves on the way who was the greatest. Then he sat down, called the Twelve, and said to them, "If anyone wishes to be first, he shall be the last of all and the servant of all." Taking a child, he placed it in their midst, and putting his arms around it, he said to them, "Whoever receives one child such as this in my name, receives me; and whoever receives me, receives not me but the One who sent me."

***First Reading* (Wis 2:12, 17-20)**

The wicked say:
Let us beset the just one, because he is obnoxious to us;
he sets himself against our doings,
Reproaches us for transgressions of the law
and charges us with violations of our training.
Let us see whether his words be true;
let us find out what will happen to him.
For if the just one be the son of God, God will defend him
and deliver him from the hand of his foes.
With revilement and torture let us put the just one to the test
that we may have proof of his gentleness
and try his patience.
Let us condemn him to a shameful death;
for according to his own words, God will take care of him.

Responsorial Psalm (Ps 54:3-4, 5, 6-8)

℟. (6b) The Lord upholds my life.

O God, by your name save me,
  and by your might defend my cause.
O God, hear my prayer;
  hearken to the words of my mouth.

℟. The Lord upholds my life.

For the haughty men have risen up against me,
  the ruthless seek my life;
  they set not God before their eyes.

℟. The Lord upholds my life.

Behold, God is my helper;
  the Lord sustains my life.
Freely will I offer you sacrifice;
  I will praise your name, O LORD, for its goodness.

℟. The Lord upholds my life.

Second Reading (Jas 3:16–4:3)

Reflecting on Living the Gospel

The Twelve need to be shocked out of their competitiveness and power-seeking. Jesus does what would be almost inconceivable in first-century Palestinian culture, where children, along with women and slaves, had almost no social status. In front of his twelve adult male disciples, Jesus wraps his arms around a disregarded child. Here "inside the house," a symbol of the domestic church, is a parable in action which teaches that what should characterize the ecclesial household is inclusion and equality, not exclusion and superiority.

Connecting the Responsorial Psalm to the Readings

We find the humility that Jesus expects from his followers expressed in today's responsorial psalm. Rather than boasting of one's accomplishments and self-sufficiency, the psalmist points to the One who holds all human life in his hands, singing, "The Lord upholds my life." In today's gospel Jesus calls a child forward, telling the disciples, "Whoever receives one child such as this in my name, receives me." Jesus lavishes attention on the child not because of his or her innocence or spiritual capacity, but because of the child's utter dependence on others. In our own day and age, children continue to be the most vulnerable of society, relying on others for food, shelter, affection, and education. As Christians, we are called to serve the vulnerable and to be willing to be vulnerable ourselves.

Psalmist Preparation

Instead of focusing on our own supposed "greatness," we must shift our gaze to the One who is our "helper" and sustainer, the One who is worthy of all praise. How do you embrace humility as part of your spiritual path?

Prayer

God of eternity,
your promises are true and everlasting, your Spirit fills all creation.
Your love, manifest in your son and his sacrificial life,
upholds my life and fills me with wonder and awe.
I, with all those you love, praise you and
thank you for your kindness and divine presence. Amen.

TWENTY-SIXTH SUNDAY IN ORDINARY TIME

SEPTEMBER 26, 2021

***Gospel* (Mark 9:38-43, 45, 47-48; L137B)**

At that time, John said to Jesus, "Teacher, we saw someone driving out demons in your name, and we tried to prevent him because he does not follow us." Jesus replied, "Do not prevent him. There is no one who performs a mighty deed in my name who can at the same time speak ill of me. For whoever is not against us is for us. Anyone who gives you a cup of water to drink because you belong to Christ, amen, I say to you, will surely not lose his reward.

"Whoever causes one of these little ones who believe in me to sin, it would be better for him if a great millstone were put around his neck and he were thrown into the sea. If your hand causes you to sin, cut it off. It is better for you to enter into life maimed than with two hands to go into Gehenna, into the unquenchable fire. And if your foot causes you to sin, cut if off. It is better for you to enter into life crippled than with two feet to be thrown into Gehenna. And if your eye causes you to sin, pluck it out. Better for you to enter into the kingdom of God with one eye than with two eyes to be thrown into Gehenna, where 'their worm does not die, and the fire is not quenched.'"

***First Reading* (Num 11:25-29)**

The Lord came down in the cloud and spoke to Moses. Taking some of the spirit that was on Moses, the Lord bestowed it on the seventy elders; and as the spirit came to rest on them, they prophesied.

Now two men, one named Eldad and the other Medad, were not in the gathering but had been left in the camp. They too had been on the list, but had not gone out to the tent; yet the spirit came to rest on them also, and they prophesied in the camp. So, when a young man quickly told Moses, "Eldad and Medad are prophesying in the camp," Joshua, son of Nun, who from his youth had been Moses' aide, said, "Moses, my lord, stop them." But Moses answered him, "Are you jealous for my sake? Would that all the people of the Lord were prophets! Would that the Lord might bestow his spirit on them all!"

TWENTY-SIXTH SUNDAY IN ORDINARY TIME

***Responsorial Psalm* (Ps 19:8, 10, 12-13, 14)**

℟. (9a) The precepts of the Lord give joy to the heart.

The law of the LORD is perfect,
  refreshing the soul;
the decree of the LORD is trustworthy,
  giving wisdom to the simple.

℟. The precepts of the Lord give joy to the heart.

The fear of the LORD is pure,
  enduring forever;
the ordinances of the LORD are true,
  all of them just.

℟. The precepts of the Lord give joy to the heart.

Though your servant is careful of them,
  very diligent in keeping them,
yet who can detect failings?
  Cleanse me from my unknown faults!

℟. The precepts of the Lord give joy to the heart.

From wanton sin especially, restrain your servant;
  let it not rule over me.
Then shall I be blameless and innocent
  of serious sin.

℟. The precepts of the Lord give joy to the heart.

***Second Reading* (Jas 5:1-6)**

Reflecting on Living the Gospel

Strong feelings evoke strong language, and the Markan Jesus uses vivid images to heighten the impact of his words about the sin and scandal of those who are a stumbling block to the faith of others. Rather than concentrate on criticizing those whom we consider "outsiders," disciples need to be self-critical. The harsh words about self-mutilation are to be taken figuratively, not literally. It would be better, says Jesus, to go through life physically handicapped than to give scandal by our sinfulness, making us unfit for the kingdom of God.

Connecting the Responsorial Psalm to the Readings

Today's psalm combines praise and repentance. Rather than a burden, the law of the Lord is hailed as a gift that brings refreshment, wisdom, and purity to those who seek to walk in its ways. And yet, even for one who takes delight in God's law, divine assistance is necessary. The psalmist requests the Lord to "[c]leanse me from my unknown faults" and to "restrain" him or her "from wanton sin."

Psalmist Preparation

In this psalm we find that holiness is first of all about love of God. When we worship God with our whole hearts, minds, and spirits, our one desire is to remain in close relationship with him. Anything that might separate us from this intimacy with God is rightly seen as an evil to be rejected at once. How does living within the precepts of the Lord bring joy to your own heart?

Prayer

God of the prophets, God of the law,
your *precepts give joy to the heart.*
Yet, without love, your laws are cold and harsh.
Love too is fickle outside of your commands.
Make us always mindful of both your laws and your love,
you who live and reign forever and ever. Amen.

TWENTY-SEVENTH SUNDAY IN ORDINARY TIME

Gospel (Mark 10:2-16 [or 10:2-12]; L140B)

The Pharisees approached Jesus and asked, "Is it lawful for a husband to divorce his wife?" They were testing him. He said to them in reply, "What did Moses command you?" They replied, "Moses permitted a husband to write a bill of divorce and dismiss her." But Jesus told them, "Because of the hardness of your hearts he wrote you this commandment. But from the beginning of creation, *God made them male and female. For this reason a man shall leave his father and mother and be joined to his wife, and the two shall become one flesh.* So they are no longer two but one flesh. Therefore what God has joined together, no human being must separate." In the house the disciples again questioned Jesus about this. He said to them, "Whoever divorces his wife and marries another commits adultery against her; and if she divorces her husband and marries another, she commits adultery."

And people were bringing children to him that he might touch them, but the disciples rebuked them. When Jesus saw this he became indignant and said to them, "Let the children come to me; do not prevent them, for the kingdom of God belongs to such as these. Amen, I say to you, whoever does not accept the kingdom of God like a child will not enter it." Then he embraced them and blessed them, placing his hands on them.

First Reading (Gen 2:18-24)

The LORD God said: "It is not good for the man to be alone. I will make a suitable partner for him." So the LORD God formed out of the ground various wild animals and various birds of the air, and he brought them to the man to see what he would call them; whatever the man called each of them would be its name. The man gave names to all the cattle, all the birds of the air, and all wild animals; but none proved to be the suitable partner for the man.

So the LORD God cast a deep sleep on the man, and while he was asleep, he took out one of his ribs and closed up its place with flesh. The LORD God then built up into a woman the rib that he had taken from the man. When he brought her to the man, the man said: / "This one, at last, is bone of my bones / and flesh of my flesh; / this one shall be called 'woman,' / for out of 'her man' this one has been taken." / That is why a man leaves his father and mother and clings to his wife, and the two of them become one flesh.

Responsorial Psalm **(Ps 128:1-2, 3, 4-5, 6)**

℟. (cf. 5) May the Lord bless us all the days of our lives.

Blessed are you who fear the LORD,
  who walk in his ways!
For you shall eat the fruit of your handiwork;
  blessed shall you be, and favored.

℟. May the Lord bless us all the days of our lives.

Your wife shall be like a fruitful vine
  in the recesses of your home;
your children like olive plants
  around your table.

℟. May the Lord bless us all the days of our lives.

Behold, thus is the man blessed
  who fears the LORD.
The LORD bless you from Zion:
  may you see the prosperity of Jerusalem
  all the days of your life.

℟. May the Lord bless us all the days of our lives.

May you see your children's children.
  Peace be upon Israel!

℟. May the Lord bless us all the days of our lives.

Second Reading **(Heb 2:9-11)**

Reflecting on Living the Gospel

We should not hear this gospel as a sentimental romanticizing or idealizing of children, but as an embrace of Jesus for all those who have no status, no claims to make, no power to wield, and so are receptive to the great gift that is offered—the kingdom of God. With what have we been touched: with the distorted hope of the disciples for power, or with willingness to be "little ones" who are open to and receptive of the reigning presence of God?

TWENTY-SEVENTH SUNDAY IN ORDINARY TIME

Connecting the Responsorial Psalm to the Readings

Today's gospel reading focuses on both the importance of marriage and the importance of children. Whatever our vocation—whether to ordained or consecrated life, single life, or marriage—as human beings we crave community. In today's psalm, the blessings of the Lord are seen tangibly present in a family gathered around a household table, and prosperity is to live a long life and eventually see "your children's children."

Psalmist Preparation

Whatever your vocation, who is the family that gathers around your table and how do you find God in communion with others?

Prayer

Generous God,
your gifts of life, love, and happiness are all around us.
When it is difficult to perceive them, to perceive you,
increase our faith, and bring us more deeply into your community of believers.
In these and all other ways, we pray:
bless us all the days of our lives. Amen.

TWENTY-EIGHTH SUNDAY IN ORDINARY TIME

OCTOBER 10, 2021

***Gospel* (Mark 10:17-30 [or 10:17-27]; L143B)**

As Jesus was setting out on a journey, a man ran up, knelt down before him, and asked him, "Good teacher, what must I do to inherit eternal life?" Jesus answered him, "Why do you call me good? No one is good but God alone. You know the commandments: *You shall not kill; you shall not commit adultery; you shall not steal; you shall not bear false witness; you shall not defraud; honor your father and your mother.*" He replied and said to him, "Teacher, all of these I have observed from my youth." Jesus, looking at him, loved him and said to him, "You are lacking in one thing. Go, sell what you have, and give to the poor and you will have treasure in heaven; then come, follow me." At that statement his face fell, and he went away sad, for he had many possessions.

Jesus looked around and said to his disciples, "How hard it is for those who have wealth to enter the kingdom of God!" The disciples were amazed at his words. So Jesus again said to them in reply, "Children, how hard it is to enter the kingdom of God! It is easier for a camel to pass through the eye of a needle than for one who is rich to enter the kingdom of God." They were exceedingly astonished and said among themselves, "Then who can be saved?" Jesus looked at them and said, "For human beings it is impossible, but not for God. All things are possible for God." Peter began to say to him, "We have given up everything and followed you." Jesus said, "Amen, I say to you, there is no one who has given up house or brothers or sisters or mother or father or children or lands for my sake and for the sake of the gospel who will not receive a hundred times more now in this present age: houses and brothers and sisters and mothers and children and lands, with persecutions, and eternal life in the age to come."

TWENTY-EIGHTH SUNDAY IN ORDINARY TIME

***First Reading* (Wis 7:7-11)**

I prayed, and prudence was given me;
  I pleaded, and the spirit of wisdom came to me.
I preferred her to scepter and throne,
and deemed riches nothing in comparison with her,
  nor did I liken any priceless gem to her;
because all gold, in view of her, is a little sand,
  and before her, silver is to be accounted mire.
Beyond health and comeliness I loved her,
and I chose to have her rather than the light,
  because the splendor of her never yields to sleep.
Yet all good things together came to me in her company,
  and countless riches at her hands.

***Responsorial Psalm* (Ps 90:12-13, 14-15, 16-17)**

℟. (14) Fill us with your love, O Lord, and we will sing for joy!

Teach us to number our days aright,
  that we may gain wisdom of heart.
Return, O LORD! How long?
  Have pity on your servants!

℟. Fill us with your love, O Lord, and we will sing for joy!

Fill us at daybreak with your kindness,
  that we may shout for joy and gladness all our days.
Make us glad, for the days when you afflicted us,
  for the years when we saw evil.

℟. Fill us with your love, O Lord, and we will sing for joy!

Let your work be seen by your servants
  and your glory by their children;
and may the gracious care of the Lord our God be ours;
  prosper the work of our hands for us!
  Prosper the work of our hands!

℟. Fill us with your love, O Lord, and we will sing for joy!

***Second Reading* (Heb 4:12-13)**

Reflecting on Living the Gospel

Jesus assures Peter that those who give up the "everything" of possessions and relationships for the sake of following him and the gospel with which he identifies himself will receive a hundredfold: new relationships in the new family of Jesus's followers, new possessions that are the fruit of doing and hearing the word of God and, the most cherished possession of all, the eternal life they had witnessed the man was seeking. But with all these benefits will come persecution, for no disciple can escape the Cross.

Connecting the Responsorial Psalm to the Readings

Today's responsorial psalm calls upon the generosity of God to "[f]ill us with your love, O Lord, and we will sing for joy!" In Christ, not only are we called to become more than we previously were, but we are also given the help and strength necessary for transformation. Only with God's wisdom and compassion are we able to "number our days aright" and to know what is truly worthy of our time, attention, and labors. When we understand the preciousness of life in Christ, all else becomes unimportant and it is easy to leave behind that which saps our energies and leads us away from God's love.

Psalmist Preparation

Where do you find your deepest joy? How does this guide you to a closer relationship with Jesus?

Prayer

God of creativity,
we pray today that we be empty vessels,
ready to be filled by your love, your riches, your presence.
We will sing for joy when filled to bursting.
We cannot help but overflow your praises
in exuberant, joyful tones. Amen.

TWENTY-NINTH SUNDAY IN ORDINARY TIME

***Gospel* (Mark 10:35-45 [or 10:42-45]; L146B)**

James and John, the sons of Zebedee, came to Jesus and said to him, "Teacher, we want you to do for us whatever we ask of you." He replied, "What do you wish me to do for you?" They answered him, "Grant that in your glory we may sit one at your right and the other at your left." Jesus said to them, "You do not know what you are asking. Can you drink the cup that I drink or be baptized with the baptism with which I am baptized?" They said to him, "We can." Jesus said to them, "The cup that I drink, you will drink, and with the baptism with which I am baptized, you will be baptized; but to sit at my right or at my left is not mine to give but is for those for whom it has been prepared." When the ten heard this, they became indignant at James and John. Jesus summoned them and said to them, "You know that those who are recognized as rulers over the Gentiles lord it over them, and their great ones make their authority over them felt. But it shall not be so among you. Rather, whoever wishes to be great among you will be your servant; whoever wishes to be first among you will be the slave of all. For the Son of Man did not come to be served but to serve and to give his life as a ransom for many."

***First Reading* (Isa 53:10-11)**

The LORD was pleased
to crush him in infirmity.

If he gives his life as an offering for sin,
he shall see his descendants in a long life,
and the will of the LORD shall be accomplished through him.

Because of his affliction
he shall see the light in fullness of days;
Through his suffering, my servant shall justify many,
and their guilt he shall bear.

***Responsorial Psalm* (Ps 33:4-5, 18-19, 20 and 22)**

℟. (22) Lord, let your mercy be on us, as we place our trust in you.

Upright is the word of the LORD,
  and all his works are trustworthy.
He loves justice and right;
  of the kindness of the LORD the earth is full.

℟. Lord, let your mercy be on us, as we place our trust in you.

See, the eyes of the LORD are upon those who fear him,
  upon those who hope for his kindness,
To deliver them from death
  and preserve them in spite of famine.

℟. Lord, let your mercy be on us, as we place our trust in you.

Our soul waits for the LORD,
  who is our help and our shield.
May your kindness, O LORD, be upon us
  who have put our hope in you.

℟. Lord, let your mercy be on us, as we place our trust in you.

***Second Reading* (Heb 4:14-16)**

Reflecting on Living the Gospel

The failure of his disciples to understand him, his mission, or his relationship to his Father was an aspect of Jesus's suffering. Their desertion on the eve of his passion would add to the bitterness of the cup he would drink. Power and triumphalism, the desire for first places in the kingdom, have nothing to do with Christian leadership, yet into the hands of these frail and failing human beings Jesus entrusts the Christian community. This is both our challenge and our consolation.

Connecting the Responsorial Psalm to the Readings

In the second reading, the author of the letter to the Hebrews assures us that we have nothing to fear since "we do not have a high priest / who is unable to sympathize with our weaknesses, / but one who has similarly been tested in every way, / yet without sin." In Jesus's ability to empathize with our human struggles, we find another reason to agree with the psalmist's proclamation: "Upright is the word of the Lord, / and all his works are trustworthy." In the midst of life's trials, we turn to the Lord "who is our help and our shield."

TWENTY-NINTH SUNDAY IN ORDINARY TIME

Psalmist Preparation

In your own life, how have you experienced the Lord as "trustworthy" in times of hardship?

Prayer

Merciful Love,
you have always been patient
when we, your people, neglect you and your covenant.
At times we may feel unworthy,
but you are always ready to welcome the return of a repentant heart.
Let your mercy be on us, as we place our trust in you. Amen.

THIRTIETH SUNDAY IN ORDINARY TIME

OCTOBER 24, 2021

Gospel **(Mark 10:46-52; L149B)**

As Jesus was leaving Jericho with his disciples and a sizable crowd, Bartimaeus, a blind man, the son of Timaeus, sat by the roadside begging. On hearing that it was Jesus of Nazareth, he began to cry out and say, "Jesus, son of David, have pity on me." And many rebuked him, telling him to be silent. But he kept calling out all the more, "Son of David, have pity on me." Jesus stopped and said, "Call him." So they called the blind man, saying to him, "Take courage; get up, Jesus is calling you." He threw aside his cloak, sprang up, and came to Jesus. Jesus said to him in reply, "What do you want me to do for you?" The blind man replied to him, "Master, I want to see." Jesus told him, "Go your way; your faith has saved you." Immediately he received his sight and followed him on the way.

First Reading **(Jer 31:7-9)**

Thus says the LORD:
Shout with joy for Jacob,
  exult at the head of the nations;
  proclaim your praise and say:
The LORD has delivered his people,
  the remnant of Israel.
Behold, I will bring them back
  from the land of the north;
I will gather them from the ends of the world,
  with the blind and the lame in their midst,
the mothers and those with child;
  they shall return as an immense throng.
They departed in tears,
  but I will console them and guide them;
I will lead them to brooks of water,
  on a level road, so that none shall stumble.
For I am a father to Israel,
  Ephraim is my first-born.

THIRTIETH SUNDAY IN ORDINARY TIME

***Responsorial Psalm* (Ps 126:1-2ab, 2cd-3, 4-5, 6)**

℟. (3) The Lord has done great things for us; we are filled with joy.

When the LORD brought back the captives of Zion,
we were like men dreaming.
Then our mouth was filled with laughter,
and our tongue with rejoicing.

℟. The Lord has done great things for us; we are filled with joy.

Then they said among the nations,
"The LORD has done great things for them."
The LORD has done great things for us;
we are glad indeed.

℟. The Lord has done great things for us; we are filled with joy.

Restore our fortunes, O LORD,
like the torrents in the southern desert.
Those that sow in tears
shall reap rejoicing.

℟. The Lord has done great things for us; we are filled with joy.

Although they go forth weeping,
carrying the seed to be sown,
They shall come back rejoicing,
carrying their sheaves.

℟. The Lord has done great things for us; we are filled with joy.

***Second Reading* (Heb 5:1-6)**

Reflecting on Living the Gospel

Are we aware of our own blindness, of our inability to recognize Jesus who is passing through our everyday lives? Do we urgently ask for insightful faith so that we recognize who Jesus really is? Or are we reluctant to leave even the small, secure territory that we have staked out for ourselves and push forward to Jesus, ready to enter with him into whatever "Jerusalem" he will lead us into, with his promise of a share in his passion, death . . . and resurrection?

Connecting the Responsorial Psalm to the Readings

Today's psalm echoes the gladness of Jeremiah's prophecy. The people who have been restored to their homeland sing, "The Lord has done great things for us; we are filled with joy." In today's readings we see God's saving power in the life of a nation and in the life of an individual in need of healing. Our God continues to interact with us this way. We are saved in community as the people of God, the Body of Christ, but we are also cared for as beloved sons and daughters. We continue to read the Sacred Scriptures to remember the history of God's redemptive relationship with people throughout the ages, but also because it calls us to recognize God's movement in our own lives. Today's psalm reminds us that though we might at times "sow in tears," we will eventually "reap rejoicing."

Psalmist Preparation

In your life of faith, how do you celebrate and remember the great things God has done for you?

Prayer

God of wonders,
our hearts soar as we recall your inbreaking into our human time
and space,
over and over again,
to share your love of us and offer us redemption.
Mindful that you have *done great things for us,*
we are filled with joy. Amen.

THIRTY-FIRST SUNDAY IN ORDINARY TIME

***Gospel* (Mark 12:28b-34; L152B)**

One of the scribes came to Jesus and asked him, "Which is the first of all the commandments?" Jesus replied, "The first is this: *Hear, O Israel! The Lord our God is Lord alone! You shall love the Lord your God with all your heart, with all your soul, with all your mind, and with all your strength.* The second is this: *You shall love your neighbor as yourself.* There is no other commandment greater than these." The scribe said to him, "Well said, teacher. You are right in saying, 'He is One and there is no other than he.' And 'to love him with all your heart, with all your understanding, with all your strength, and to love your neighbor as yourself' is worth more than all burnt offerings and sacrifices." And when Jesus saw that he answered with understanding, he said to him, "You are not far from the kingdom of God." And no one dared to ask him any more questions.

***First Reading* (Deut 6:2-6)**

Moses spoke to the people, saying: "Fear the LORD, your God, and keep, throughout the days of your lives, all his statutes and commandments which I enjoin on you, and thus have long life. Hear then, Israel, and be careful to observe them, that you may grow and prosper the more, in keeping with the promise of the LORD, the God of your fathers, to give you a land flowing with milk and honey.

"Hear, O Israel! The LORD is our God, the LORD alone! Therefore, you shall love the LORD, your God, with all your heart, and with all your soul, and with all your strength. Take to heart these words which I enjoin on you today."

***Responsorial Psalm* (Ps 18:2-3, 3-4, 47, 51)**

℟. (2) I love you, Lord, my strength.

I love you, O LORD, my strength,
O LORD, my rock, my fortress, my deliverer.

℟. I love you, Lord, my strength.

My God, my rock of refuge,
my shield, the horn of my salvation, my stronghold!
Praised be the LORD, I exclaim,
and I am safe from my enemies.

℟. I love you, Lord, my strength.

The LORD lives! And blessed be my rock!
Extolled be God my savior,
you who gave great victories to your king
and showed kindness to your anointed.

℟. I love you, Lord, my strength.

***Second Reading* (Heb 7:23-28)**

Reflecting on Living the Gospel

The meeting of Jesus and the scribe becomes an enactment of the great commandment of love. They treat each other as neighbors, transcending party politics and religious differences, crossing the dividing line between "you" and "us." In the sea of hostility that Mark describes in this chapter of his gospel, the mutual affirmation of Jesus and the scribe is like an island of reconciliation. It has much to say to us, as individuals or communities, about the course we should set in daily relationships or in ecumenical and interfaith dialogue.

Connecting the Responsorial Psalm to the Readings

Moses tells the people, "[Y]ou shall love the LORD, your God, . . . with all your soul, and with all your strength." Today's responsorial psalm points to the Lord as the source of this strength. God is hailed as rock, fortress, and deliverer. Our strength comes from the firm foundation of the covenant relationship with our Creator. All good gifts we receive from the Lord, including the ability to love and serve him with fidelity. When our faith wavers or our love weakens, we can always turn to the One who is our shield, salvation, and stronghold for help and renewal.

THIRTY-FIRST SUNDAY IN ORDINARY TIME

Psalmist Preparation

Where are you in need of God's strength to help you live with fidelity the commandments to love God and love neighbor?

Prayer

Mighty One,
I love you, Lord, my strength.
You are a rock of refuge for me, and for all who seek shelter.
When enemies surround and storms arise,
your mantle protects us and keeps us safe.
Help us be ever mindful of your caring presence. Amen.

NOVEMBER 1, 2021

***Gospel* (Matt 5:1-12a; L667)**

When Jesus saw the crowds, he went up the mountain, and after he had sat down, his disciples came to him. He began to teach them, saying:

"Blessed are the poor in spirit,
for theirs is the Kingdom of heaven.
Blessed are they who mourn,
for they will be comforted.
Blessed are the meek,
for they will inherit the land.
Blessed are they who hunger and thirst
for righteousness,
for they will be satisfied.
Blessed are the merciful,
for they will be shown mercy.
Blessed are the clean of heart,
for they will see God.
Blessed are the peacemakers,
for they will be called children of God.
Blessed are they who are persecuted for the sake of righteousness,
for theirs is the Kingdom of heaven.

Blessed are you when they insult you and persecute you and utter every kind of evil against you falsely because of me. Rejoice and be glad, for your reward will be great in heaven."

***First Reading* (Rev 7:2-4, 9-14)**

I, John, saw another angel come up from the East, holding the seal of the living God. He cried out in a loud voice to the four angels who were given power to damage the land and the sea, "Do not damage the land or the sea or the trees until we put the seal on the foreheads of the servants of our God." I heard the number of those who had been marked with the seal, one hundred and forty-four thousand marked from every tribe of the children of Israel.

After this I had a vision of a great multitude, which no one could count, from every nation, race, people, and tongue. They stood before the throne and before the Lamb, wearing white robes and holding palm branches in their hands. They cried out in a loud voice:

"Salvation comes from our God,
who is seated on the throne,
and from the Lamb."

All the angels stood around the throne and around the elders and the four living creatures. They prostrated themselves before the throne, worshiped God, and exclaimed:

"Amen. Blessing and glory, wisdom and thanksgiving,
honor, power, and might
be to our God forever and ever. Amen."

Then one of the elders spoke up and said to me, "Who are these wearing white robes, and where did they come from?" I said to him, "My lord, you are the one who knows." He said to me, "These are the ones who have survived the time of great distress; they have washed their robes and made them white in the Blood of the Lamb."

***Responsorial Psalm* (Ps 24:1bc-2, 3-4ab, 5-6)**

℟. (cf. 6) Lord, this is the people that longs to see your face.

The LORD's are the earth and its fullness;
the world and those who dwell in it.
For he founded it upon the seas
and established it upon the rivers.

℟. Lord, this is the people that longs to see your face.

Who can ascend the mountain of the LORD?
or who may stand in his holy place?
One whose hands are sinless, whose heart is clean,
who desires not what is vain.

℟. Lord, this is the people that longs to see your face.

He shall receive a blessing from the LORD,
a reward from God his savior.
Such is the race that seeks for him,
that seeks the face of the God of Jacob.

℟. Lord, this is the people that longs to see your face.

See Appendix, p. 208, for Second Reading

Reflecting on Living the Gospel

The call for Christians to live up to their baptismal call ought to be a constant reminder that not only are we called *to be* saints, but, as St. Paul says, we *are* saints, however imperfectly we are running the race to the heavenly goal. It's not just that we do not share in the eternal joy of heaven now, but that we know how often we fall short of the holiness that Jesus calls us to in this life, whether in purity of heart, mercy, righteousness, or peacefulness.

Connecting the Responsorial Psalm to the Readings

In today's psalm response we pray with hope and humility, "Lord, this is the people that longs to see your face." On this holy day, we join together with the "great multitude" described in the first reading to offer praise and glory to our God, and also to experience ourselves as one of these holy ones whose deepest longing is to behold the face of God. In the gospel, Jesus tells us what is required of those who harbor this desire: "Blessed are the clean of heart," he counsels, "for they will see God." How are we to attain this cleanliness? In the second reading from the first letter of Saint John we find the answer: "Everyone who has this hope based on him makes himself pure, as he is pure."

Psalmist Preparation

How have you experienced hope as an agent of transformation and conversion on your journey of faith?

Prayer

Lord,
this is the people that longs to see your face.
Yet, who may stand in your presence,
you who are overwhelming truth, beauty, and love?
Show us signs of you all around us,
foretastes of the far-off day
when we come fully into your divine presence. Amen.

THIRTY-SECOND SUNDAY IN ORDINARY TIME

***Gospel* (Mark 12:38-44 [or 12:41-44]; L155B)**

In the course of his teaching Jesus said to the crowds, "Beware of the scribes, who like to go around in long robes and accept greetings in the marketplaces, seats of honor in synagogues, and places of honor at banquets. They devour the houses of widows and, as a pretext recite lengthy prayers. They will receive a very severe condemnation."

He sat down opposite the treasury and observed how the crowd put money into the treasury. Many rich people put in large sums. A poor widow also came and put in two small coins worth a few cents. Calling his disciples to himself, he said to them, "Amen, I say to you, this poor widow put in more than all the other contributors to the treasury. For they have all contributed from their surplus wealth, but she, from her poverty, has contributed all she had, her whole livelihood."

***First Reading* (1 Kgs 17:10-16)**

In those days, Elijah the prophet went to Zarephath. As he arrived at the entrance of the city, a widow was gathering sticks there; he called out to her, "Please bring me a small cupful of water to drink." She left to get it, and he called out after her, "Please bring along a bit of bread." She answered, "As the LORD, your God, lives, I have nothing baked; there is only a handful of flour in my jar and a little oil in my jug. Just now I was collecting a couple of sticks, to go in and prepare something for myself and my son; when we have eaten it, we shall die." Elijah said to her, "Do not be afraid. Go and do as you propose. But first make me a little cake and bring it to me. Then you can prepare something for yourself and your son. For the LORD, the God of Israel, says, 'The jar of flour shall not go empty, nor the jug of oil run dry, until the day when the LORD sends rain upon the earth.'" She left and did as Elijah had said. She was able to eat for a year, and he and her son as well; the jar of flour did not go empty, nor the jug of oil run dry, as the LORD had foretold through Elijah.

***Responsorial Psalm* (Ps 146:7, 8-9, 9-10)**

℟. (1b) Praise the Lord, my soul! *or:* ℟. Alleluia.

The LORD keeps faith forever,
secures justice for the oppressed,
gives food to the hungry.
The LORD sets captives free.

℟. Praise the Lord, my soul! *or:* ℟. Alleluia.

The LORD gives sight to the blind;
the LORD raises up those who were bowed down.
The LORD loves the just;
the LORD protects strangers.

℟. Praise the Lord, my soul! *or:* ℟. Alleluia.

The fatherless and the widow he sustains,
but the way of the wicked he thwarts.
The LORD shall reign forever;
your God, O Zion, through all generations. Alleluia.

℟. Praise the Lord, my soul! *or:* ℟. Alleluia.

***Second Reading* (Heb 9:24-28)**

Reflecting on Living the Gospel

We should not read into this gospel a romanticization of poverty nor a condemnation of large donations. It is the motivation behind gifts, large or small, that is important. To give out of our surplus may be useful for taxation purposes, or a generous donation may be great publicity for the corporate business image. We may be able to think of ways the church is not exempt from such temptations. It is acting out of love that makes the difference in the eyes of God.

Connecting the Responsorial Psalm to the Readings

Today's psalm lifts up the privileged place of the oppressed, captive, hungry, and blind, as well as of the stranger, the widow, and the fatherless in the eyes of God. These individuals, who are so often pushed to the margins of society where they can be ignored by those who do not know their struggles, are at the center of God's attention and care. In the first reading and the gospel, we also see how God values the contributions of those considered powerless. Elijah calls upon a widow to feed him when he enters Zarephath, and Jesus lauds the contribution of the poor widow, who gives "all she had, / her whole livelihood."

Psalmist Preparation

How do you and your faith community support the poor and oppressed? And how do you welcome and celebrate the gifts they bring?

Prayer

God of all,
make strong in us a sense of belonging to your holy family.
So too, show us prodigiously your love for each of us,
with a zeal that knows no bounds.
In the warmth and energy of that love, give each of us the courage
to exclaim,
Praise the Lord, my soul!

THIRTY-THIRD SUNDAY IN ORDINARY TIME

NOVEMBER 14, 2021

***Gospel* (Mark 13:24-32; L158B)**

Jesus said to his disciples: "In those days after that tribulation the sun will be darkened, and the moon will not give its light, and the stars will be falling from the sky, and the powers in the heavens will be shaken.

"And then they will see 'the Son of Man coming in the clouds' with great power and glory, and then he will send out the angels and gather his elect from the four winds, from the end of the earth to the end of the sky.

"Learn a lesson from the fig tree. When its branch becomes tender and sprouts leaves, you know that summer is near. In the same way, when you see these things happening, know that he is near, at the gates. Amen, I say to you, this generation will not pass away until all these things have taken place. Heaven and earth will pass away, but my words will not pass away.

"But of that day or hour, no one knows, neither the angels in heaven, nor the Son, but only the Father."

***First Reading* (Dan 12:1-3)**

In those days, I, Daniel, heard this word of the LORD:

"At that time there shall arise
Michael, the great prince,
guardian of your people;
It shall be a time unsurpassed in distress
since nations began until that time.
At that time your people shall escape,
everyone who is found written in the book.

"Many of those who sleep in the dust of the earth shall awake;
some shall live forever,
others shall be an everlasting horror and disgrace.

"But the wise shall shine brightly
like the splendor of the firmament,
And those who lead the many to justice
shall be like the stars forever."

THIRTY-THIRD SUNDAY IN ORDINARY TIME

***Responsorial Psalm* (Ps 16:5, 8, 9-10, 11)**

℟. (1) You are my inheritance, O Lord!

O Lord, my allotted portion and my cup,
you it is who hold fast my lot.
I set the Lord ever before me;
with him at my right hand I shall not be disturbed.

℟. You are my inheritance, O Lord!

Therefore my heart is glad and my soul rejoices,
my body, too, abides in confidence;
Because you will not abandon my soul to the netherworld,
nor will you suffer your faithful one to undergo corruption.

℟. You are my inheritance, O Lord!

You will show me the path to life,
fullness of joys in your presence,
the delights at your right hand forever.

℟. You are my inheritance, O Lord!

***Second Reading* (Heb 10:11-14, 18)**

Reflecting on Living the Gospel

Death is coming for each of us, whether we will confront it in our own personal *eschaton* or in the cosmic apocalyptic drama as described in the Gospel of Mark. Even if "the end" does not occur in our lifetime, and even if another group of end-time prophets falsely calculate Jesus's return and offer precise dates that do not come to pass, we will still come to our end. How are we preparing for it?

Connecting the Responsorial Psalm to the Readings

Today's psalm offers us comfort and hope as we consider the final judgment awaiting each of us. Our Lord is perfectly just and perfectly merciful, and in his mercy he holds us safe, where we might abide "in confidence" knowing the Lord "will not abandon my soul to the netherworld, / nor . . . suffer your faithful one to undergo corruption." When we rely on the Lord as our "inheritance" and dedicate our lives to serving and loving him, we need not fear "everlasting horror and disgrace." We hold fast to the words Jesus has spoken, knowing that "[h]eaven and earth will pass away, / but [his] words will not pass away."

Psalmist Preparation

Today's psalm looks forward to "fullness of joys in [God's] presence." How does the joy of God fill your life at this moment?

Prayer

God of all good gifts,
each of us, great and small, are your adopted children.
You bestow upon us all we ever need
to grow in holiness and to one day be with you eternally.
We cry, *you are my inheritance, O Lord!*

OUR LORD JESUS CHRIST, KING OF THE UNIVERSE

***Gospel* (John 18:33b-37; L161B)**

Pilate said to Jesus, "Are you the King of the Jews?" Jesus answered, "Do you say this on your own or have others told you about me?" Pilate answered, "I am not a Jew, am I? Your own nation and the chief priests handed you over to me. What have you done?" Jesus answered, "My kingdom does not belong to this world. If my kingdom did belong to this world, my attendants would be fighting to keep me from being handed over to the Jews. But as it is, my kingdom is not here." So Pilate said to him, "Then you are a king?" Jesus answered, "You say I am a king. For this I was born and for this I came into the world, to testify to the truth. Everyone who belongs to the truth listens to my voice."

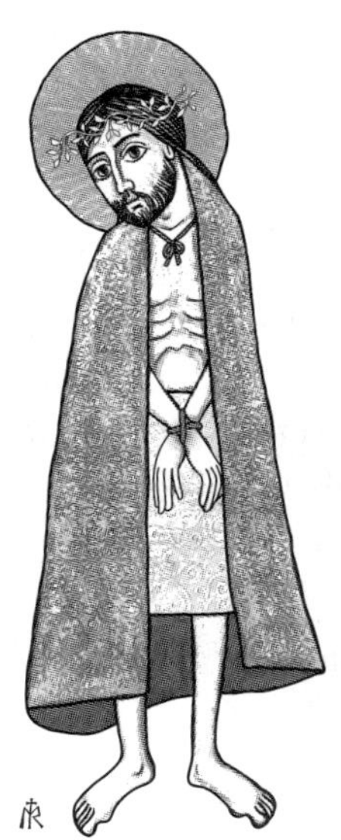

***First Reading* (Dan 7:13-14)**

As the visions during the night continued, I saw
one like a Son of man coming,
on the clouds of heaven;
When he reached the Ancient One
and was presented before him,
the one like a Son of man received dominion, glory, and kingship;
all peoples, nations, and languages serve him.
His dominion is an everlasting dominion
that shall not be taken away,
his kingship shall not be destroyed.

***Responsorial Psalm* (Ps 93:1, 1-2, 5)**

℟. (1a) The Lord is king; he is robed in majesty.

The LORD is king, in splendor robed;
robed is the LORD and girt about with strength.

℟. The Lord is king; he is robed in majesty.

And he has made the world firm,
  not to be moved.
Your throne stands firm from of old;
  from everlasting you are, O LORD.

℟. The Lord is king; he is robed in majesty.

Your decrees are worthy of trust indeed;
  holiness befits your house,
  O LORD, for length of days.

℟. The Lord is king; he is robed in majesty.

See Appendix, p. 208, for Second Reading

Reflecting on Living the Gospel

Is our God cozy or cosmic? That is the large and exciting question that challenges us on this last Sunday of the liturgical year as we celebrate the solemnity of Christ the King. It is the celebration of the climax, not only of this year of grace, but also of the end, the omega point of the mystery toward which we orient our lives. Behind Christ is the God who reveals himself in Christ, the "I AM" who is the Alpha and the Omega, the Beginning and the End.

Connecting the Responsorial Psalm to the Readings

Today's responsorial psalm sings to the Lord, who "is king, he is robed in majesty." Our praise and worship of God, the almighty, gives us hope and trust in the world God has made, which is "firm / not to be moved." God's decrees ground us, as well, on the path of salvation as we strive for holiness that "befits your house, / O Lord." While we proclaim Jesus king of creation, we also know that his kingdom goes beyond our lived reality. Jesus explains to Pilate, "My kingdom does not belong to this world." And so, as subjects of this king, we are called beyond ourselves, to grow and develop as children of God who devote their lives to service and to love.

OUR LORD JESUS CHRIST, KING OF THE UNIVERSE

Psalmist Preparation

In this coming liturgical year, how would you like to rededicate your life to Jesus, king of the universe?

Prayer

Ruler of all,
your example to us is that those who wish to lead should serve,
and that those who wish a crown should accept one made of thorns.
We pray you give us fortitude to always follow in your ways,
you who are *king, robed in majesty.* Amen.

APPENDIX

FIRST SUNDAY OF ADVENT, November 29, 2020

***Second Reading* (1 Cor 1:3-9)**

Brothers and sisters: Grace to you and peace from God our Father and the Lord Jesus Christ.

I give thanks to my God always on your account for the grace of God bestowed on you in Christ Jesus, that in him you were enriched in every way, with all discourse and all knowledge, as the testimony to Christ was confirmed among you, so that you are not lacking in any spiritual gift as you wait for the revelation of our Lord Jesus Christ. He will keep you firm to the end, irreproachable on the day of our Lord Jesus Christ. God is faithful, and by him you were called to fellowship with his Son, Jesus Christ our Lord.

SECOND SUNDAY OF ADVENT, December 6, 2020

***Second Reading* (2 Pet 3:8-14)**

Do not ignore this one fact, beloved, that with the Lord one day is like a thousand years and a thousand years like one day. The Lord does not delay his promise, as some regard "delay," but he is patient with you, not wishing that any should perish but that all should come to repentance. But the day of the Lord will come like a thief, and then the heavens will pass away with a mighty roar and the elements will be dissolved by fire, and the earth and everything done on it will be found out.

Since everything is to be dissolved in this way, what sort of persons ought you to be, conducting yourselves in holiness and devotion, waiting for and hastening the coming of the day of God, because of which the heavens will be dissolved in flames and the elements melted by fire. But according to his promise we await new heavens and a new earth in which righteousness dwells. Therefore, beloved, since you await these things, be eager to be found without spot or blemish before him, at peace.

THE IMMACULATE CONCEPTION OF THE BLESSED VIRGIN MARY, December 8, 2020

***Second Reading* (Eph 1:3-6, 11-12)**

Brothers and sisters: Blessed be the God and Father of our Lord Jesus Christ, who has blessed us in Christ with every spiritual blessing in the heavens, as he chose us in him, before the foundation of the world, to be holy and without blemish before him. In love he destined us for adoption to himself through Jesus Christ, in accord with the favor of his will, for the praise of the glory of his grace that he granted us in the beloved.

In him we were also chosen, destined in accord with the purpose of the One who accomplishes all things according to the intention of his will, so that we might exist for the praise of his glory, we who first hoped in Christ.

THIRD SUNDAY OF ADVENT, December 13, 2020
***Second Reading* (1 Thess 5:16-24)**
Brothers and sisters: Rejoice always. Pray without ceasing. In all circumstances give thanks, for this is the will of God for you in Christ Jesus. Do not quench the Spirit. Do not despise prophetic utterances. Test everything; retain what is good. Refrain from every kind of evil.

May the God of peace make you perfectly holy and may you entirely, spirit, soul, and body, be preserved blameless for the coming of our Lord Jesus Christ. The one who calls you is faithful, and he will also accomplish it.

FOURTH SUNDAY OF ADVENT, December 20, 2020
***Second Reading* (Rom 16:25-27)**
Brothers and sisters: To him who can strengthen you, according to my gospel and the proclamation of Jesus Christ, according to the revelation of the mystery kept secret for long ages but now manifested through the prophetic writings and, according to the command of the eternal God, made known to all nations to bring about the obedience of faith, to the only wise God, through Jesus Christ be glory forever and ever. Amen.

THE NATIVITY OF THE LORD, *Vigil Mass*, December 25, 2020
***Second Reading* (Acts 13:16-17, 22-25)**
When Paul reached Antioch in Pisidia and entered the synagogue, he stood up, motioned with his hand, and said, "Fellow Israelites and you others who are God-fearing, listen. The God of this people Israel chose our ancestors and exalted the people during their sojourn in the land of Egypt. With uplifted arm he led them out of it. Then he removed Saul and raised up David as king; of him he testified, 'I have found David, son of Jesse, a man after my own heart; he will carry out my every wish.' From this man's descendants God, according to his promise, has brought to Israel a savior, Jesus. John heralded his coming by proclaiming a baptism of repentance to all the people of Israel; and as John was completing his course, he would say, 'What do you suppose that I am? I am not he. Behold, one is coming after me; I am not worthy to unfasten the sandals of his feet.'"

THE NATIVITY OF THE LORD, *Mass at Midnight*, December 25, 2020
***Second Reading* (Titus 2:11-14)**
Beloved: The grace of God has appeared, saving all and training us to reject godless ways and worldly desires and to live temperately, justly, and devoutly in this age, as we await the blessed hope, the appearance of the glory of our great God and savior Jesus Christ, who gave himself for us to deliver us from all lawlessness and to cleanse for himself a people as his own, eager to do what is good.

THE NATIVITY OF THE LORD, ***Mass at Dawn,*** **December 25, 2020**
Second Reading **(Titus 3:4-7)**

Beloved:

When the kindness and generous love
of God our savior appeared,
not because of any righteous deeds we had done
but because of his mercy,
he saved us through the bath of rebirth
and renewal by the Holy Spirit,
whom he richly poured out on us
through Jesus Christ our savior,
so that we might be justified by his grace
and become heirs in hope of eternal life.

THE NATIVITY OF THE LORD, ***Mass During the Day,*** **December 25, 2020**
Second Reading **(Heb 1:1-6)**

Brothers and sisters: In times past, God spoke in partial and various ways to our ancestors through the prophets; in these last days, he has spoken to us through the Son, whom he made heir of all things and through whom he created the universe,

who is the refulgence of his glory, the very imprint of his being,
and who sustains all things by his mighty word.
When he had accomplished purification from sins,
he took his seat at the right hand of the Majesty on high,
as far superior to the angels
as the name he has inherited is more excellent than theirs.

For to which of the angels did God ever say:

You are my son; this day I have begotten you?

Or again:

I will be a father to him, and he shall be a son to me?

And again, when he leads the firstborn into the world, he says:

Let all the angels of God worship him.

THE HOLY FAMILY OF JESUS, MARY, AND JOSEPH, December 27, 2020
Second Reading **(Col 3:12-21 or 3:12-17 [or Heb 11:8, 11-12, 17-19])**

Brothers and sisters: Put on, as God's chosen ones, holy and beloved, heartfelt compassion, kindness, humility, gentleness, and patience, bearing with one another and forgiving one another, if one has a grievance against another; as the Lord has forgiven you, so must you also do. And over all these put on love, that is, the bond of perfection. And let the peace of Christ control your hearts, the peace into which you were also called in one body. And be thankful. Let the word of Christ dwell in you richly, as in all wisdom you teach and admonish one another, singing psalms, hymns, and spiritual songs with gratitude in your hearts to God. And whatever you do, in word or in deed, do everything in the name of the Lord Jesus, giving thanks to God the Father through him.

Wives, be subordinate to your husbands, as is proper in the Lord. Husbands, love your wives, and avoid any bitterness toward them. Children, obey your parents in everything, for this is pleasing to the Lord. Fathers, do not provoke your children, so they may not become discouraged.

SOLEMNITY OF MARY, THE HOLY MOTHER OF GOD, January 1, 2021
***Second Reading* (Gal 4:4-7)**

Brothers and sisters: When the fullness of time had come, God sent his Son, born of a woman, born under the law, to ransom those under the law, so that we might receive adoption as sons. As proof that you are sons, God sent the Spirit of his Son into our hearts, crying out, "Abba, Father!" So you are no longer a slave but a son, and if a son then also an heir, through God.

THE EPIPHANY OF THE LORD, January 3, 2021
***Second Reading* (Eph 3:2-3a, 5-6)**

Brothers and sisters: You have heard of the stewardship of God's grace that was given to me for your benefit, namely, that the mystery was made known to me by revelation. It was not made known to people in other generations as it has now been revealed to his holy apostles and prophets by the Spirit: that the Gentiles are coheirs, members of the same body, and copartners in the promise in Christ Jesus through the gospel.

THE BAPTISM OF THE LORD, January 10, 2021
***Second Reading* (Acts 10:34-38 [or 1 John 5:1-9])**

Peter proceeded to speak to those gathered in the house of Cornelius, saying: "In truth, I see that God shows no partiality. Rather, in every nation whoever fears him and acts uprightly is acceptable to him. You know the word that he sent to the Israelites as he proclaimed peace through Jesus Christ, who is Lord of all, what has happened all over Judea, beginning in Galilee after the baptism that John preached, how God anointed Jesus of Nazareth with the Holy Spirit and power. He went about doing good and healing all those oppressed by the devil, for God was with him."

ASH WEDNESDAY, February 17, 2021
***Second Reading* (2 Cor 5:20–6:2)**

Brothers and sisters: We are ambassadors for Christ, as if God were appealing through us. We implore you on behalf of Christ, be reconciled to God. For our sake he made him to be sin who did not know sin, so that we might become the righteousness of God in him.

Working together, then, we appeal to you not to receive the grace of God in vain. For he says:

In an acceptable time I heard you,
and on the day of salvation I helped you.

Behold, now is a very acceptable time; behold, now is the day of salvation.

FIRST SUNDAY OF LENT, February 21, 2021
***Second Reading* (1 Pet 3:18-22)**

Beloved: Christ suffered for sins once, the righteous for the sake of the unrighteous, that he might lead you to God. Put to death in the flesh, he was brought to life in the Spirit. In it he also went to preach to the spirits in prison, who had once been disobedient while God patiently waited in the days of Noah during the building of the ark, in which a few persons, eight in all, were saved through water. This prefigured baptism, which saves you now. It is not a removal of dirt from the body but an appeal to God for a clear conscience, through the resurrection of Jesus Christ, who has gone into heaven and is at the right hand of God, with angels, authorities, and powers subject to him.

SECOND SUNDAY OF LENT, February 28, 2021
***Second Reading* (Rom 8:31b-34)**

Brothers and sisters: If God is for us, who can be against us? He who did not spare his own Son but handed him over for us all, how will he not also give us everything else along with him?

Who will bring a charge against God's chosen ones? It is God who acquits us, who will condemn? Christ Jesus it is who died—or, rather, was raised—who also is at the right hand of God, who indeed intercedes for us.

THIRD SUNDAY OF LENT, March 7, 2021
***Second Reading* (1 Cor 1:22-25)**

Brothers and sisters: Jews demand signs and Greeks look for wisdom, but we proclaim Christ crucified, a stumbling block to Jews and foolishness to Gentiles, but to those who are called, Jews and Greeks alike, Christ the power of God and the wisdom of God. For the foolishness of God is wiser than human wisdom, and the weakness of God is stronger than human strength.

FOURTH SUNDAY OF LENT, March 14, 2021
***Second Reading* (Eph 2:4-10)**

Brothers and sisters: God, who is rich in mercy, because of the great love he had for us, even when we were dead in our transgressions, brought us to life with Christ—by grace you have been saved—, raised us up with him, and seated us with him in the heavens in Christ Jesus, that in the ages to come he might show the immeasurable riches of his grace in his kindness to us in Christ Jesus. For by grace you have been saved through faith, and this is not from you; it is the gift of God; it is not from works, so no one may boast. For we are his handiwork, created in Christ Jesus for the good works that God has prepared in advance, that we should live in them.

FIFTH SUNDAY OF LENT, March 21, 2021
***Second Reading* (Heb 5:7-9)**

In the days when Christ Jesus was in the flesh, he offered prayers and supplications with loud cries and tears to the one who was able to save him from death, and he was heard because of his reverence. Son though he was, he learned obedience from what he suffered; and when he was made perfect, he became the source of eternal salvation for all who obey him.

PALM SUNDAY OF THE LORD'S PASSION, March 28, 2021
***Second Reading* (Phil 2:6-11)**
Christ Jesus, though he was in the form of God,
did not regard equality with God
something to be grasped.
Rather, he emptied himself,
taking the form of a slave,
coming in human likeness;
and found human in appearance,
he humbled himself,
becoming obedient to the point of death,
even death on a cross.
Because of this, God greatly exalted him
and bestowed on him the name
which is above every name,
that at the name of Jesus
every knee should bend,
of those in heaven and on earth and under the earth,
and every tongue confess that
Jesus Christ is Lord,
to the glory of God the Father.

HOLY THURSDAY EVENING MASS OF THE LORD'S SUPPER, April 1, 2021
***Second Reading* (1 Cor 11:23-26)**
Brothers and sisters: I received from the Lord what I also handed on to you, that the Lord Jesus, on the night he was handed over, took bread, and, after he had given thanks, broke it and said, "This is my body that is for you. Do this in remembrance of me." In the same way also the cup, after supper, saying, "This cup is the new covenant in my blood. Do this, as often as you drink it, in remembrance of me." For as often as you eat this bread and drink the cup, you proclaim the death of the Lord until he comes.

FRIDAY OF THE PASSION OF THE LORD (Good Friday), April 2, 2021
***Second Reading* (Heb 4:14-16; 5:7-9)**
Brothers and sisters: Since we have a great high priest who has passed through the heavens, Jesus, the Son of God, let us hold fast to our confession. For we do not have a high priest who is unable to sympathize with our weaknesses, but one who has similarly been tested in every way, yet without sin. So let us confidently approach the throne of grace to receive mercy and to find grace for timely help.

In the days when Christ was in the flesh, he offered prayers and supplications with loud cries and tears to the one who was able to save him from death, and he was heard because of his reverence. Son though he was, he learned obedience from what he suffered; and when he was made perfect, he became the source of eternal salvation for all who obey him.

EASTER SUNDAY OF THE RESURRECTION, April 4, 2021
***Second Reading* (1 Cor 5:6b-8 [or Col 3:1-4])**
Brothers and sisters: Do you not know that a little yeast leavens all the dough? Clear out the old yeast, so that you may become a fresh batch of dough, inasmuch as you are unleavened. For our paschal lamb, Christ, has been sacrificed. Therefore, let us celebrate the feast, not with the old yeast, the yeast of malice and wickedness, but with the unleavened bread of sincerity and truth.

SECOND SUNDAY OF EASTER (or of Divine Mercy), April 11, 2021
***Second Reading* (1 John 5:1-6)**
Beloved: Everyone who believes that Jesus is the Christ is begotten by God, and everyone who loves the Father loves also the one begotten by him. In this way we know that we love the children of God when we love God and obey his commandments. For the love of God is this, that we keep his commandments. And his commandments are not burdensome, for whoever is begotten by God conquers the world. And the victory that conquers the world is our faith. Who indeed is the victor over the world but the one who believes that Jesus is the Son of God?

This is the one who came through water and blood, Jesus Christ, not by water alone, but by water and blood. The Spirit is the one that testifies, and the Spirit is truth.

THIRD SUNDAY OF EASTER, April 18, 2021
***Second Reading* (1 John 2:1-5a)**
My children, I am writing this to you so that you may not commit sin. But if anyone does sin, we have an Advocate with the Father, Jesus Christ the righteous one. He is expiation for our sins, and not for our sins only but for those of the whole world. The way we may be sure that we know him is to keep his commandments. Those who say, "I know him," but do not keep his commandments are liars, and the truth is not in them. But whoever keeps his word, the love of God is truly perfected in him.

FOURTH SUNDAY OF EASTER, April 25, 2021
***Second Reading* (1 John 3:1-2)**
Beloved: See what love the Father has bestowed on us that we may be called the children of God. Yet so we are. The reason the world does not know us is that it did not know him. Beloved, we are God's children now; what we shall be has not yet been revealed. We do know that when it is revealed we shall be like him, for we shall see him as he is.

FIFTH SUNDAY OF EASTER, May 2, 2021
***Second Reading* (1 John 3:18-24)**

Children, let us love not in word or speech but in deed and truth.

Now this is how we shall know that we belong to the truth and reassure our hearts before him in whatever our hearts condemn, for God is greater than our hearts and knows everything. Beloved, if our hearts do not condemn us, we have confidence in God and receive from him whatever we ask, because we keep his commandments and do what pleases him. And his commandment is this: we should believe in the name of his Son, Jesus Christ, and love one another just as he commanded us. Those who keep his commandments remain in him, and he in them, and the way we know that he remains in us is from the Spirit he gave us.

SIXTH SUNDAY OF EASTER, May 9, 2021
***Second Reading* (1 John 4:7-10)**

Beloved, let us love one another, because love is of God; everyone who loves is begotten by God and knows God. Whoever is without love does not know God, for God is love. In this way the love of God was revealed to us: God sent his only Son into the world so that we might have life through him. In this is love: not that we have loved God, but that he loved us and sent his Son as expiation for our sins.

THE ASCENSION OF THE LORD, May 13 or 16, 2021
***Second Reading* (Eph 4:1-13 [or Eph 1:17-23 or Eph 4:1-7, 11-13])**

Brothers and sisters, I, a prisoner for the Lord, urge you to live in a manner worthy of the call you have received, with all humility and gentleness, with patience, bearing with one another through love, striving to preserve the unity of the spirit through the bond of peace: one body and one Spirit, as you were also called to the one hope of your call; one Lord, one faith, one baptism; one God and Father of all, who is over all and through all and in all.

But grace was given to each of us according to the measure of Christ's gift. Therefore, it says:

He ascended on high and took prisoners captive;
he gave gifts to men.

What does "he ascended" mean except that he also descended into the lower regions of the earth? The one who descended is also the one who ascended far above all the heavens, that he might fill all things.

And he gave some as apostles, others as prophets, others as evangelists, others as pastors and teachers, to equip the holy ones for the work of ministry, for building up the body of Christ, until we all attain to the unity of faith and knowledge of the Son of God, to mature to manhood, to the extent of the full stature of Christ.

SEVENTH SUNDAY OF EASTER, May 16, 2021
***Second Reading* (1 John 4:11-16)**
Beloved, if God so loved us, we also must love one another. No one has ever seen God. Yet, if we love one another, God remains in us, and his love is brought to perfection in us.

This is how we know that we remain in him and he in us, that he has given us of his Spirit. Moreover, we have seen and testify that the Father sent his Son as savior of the world. Whoever acknowledges that Jesus is the Son of God, God remains in him and he in God. We have come to know and to believe in the love God has for us.

God is love, and whoever remains in love remains in God and God in him.

PENTECOST SUNDAY, May 23, 2021
***Second Reading* (Gal 5:16-25 [or 1 Cor 12:3b-7, 12-13])**
Brothers and sisters, live by the Spirit and you will certainly not gratify the desire of the flesh. For the flesh has desires against the Spirit, and the Spirit against the flesh; these are opposed to each other, so that you may not do what you want. But if you are guided by the Spirit, you are not under the law. Now the works of the flesh are obvious: immorality, impurity, lust, idolatry, sorcery, hatreds, rivalry, jealousy, outbursts of fury, acts of selfishness, dissensions, factions, occasions of envy, drinking bouts, orgies, and the like. I warn you, as I warned you before, that those who do such things will not inherit the kingdom of God. In contrast, the fruit of the Spirit is love, joy, peace, patience, kindness, generosity, faithfulness, gentleness, self-control. Against such there is no law. Now those who belong to Christ Jesus have crucified their flesh with its passions and desires. If we live in the Spirit, let us also follow the Spirit.

THE MOST HOLY TRINITY, May 30, 2021
***Second Reading* (Rom 8:14-17)**
Brothers and sisters: Those who are led by the Spirit of God are sons of God. For you did not receive a spirit of slavery to fall back into fear, but you received a Spirit of adoption, through whom we cry, "Abba, Father!" The Spirit himself bears witness with our spirit that we are children of God, and if children, then heirs, heirs of God and joint heirs with Christ, if only we suffer with him so that we may also be glorified with him.

THE MOST HOLY BODY AND BLOOD OF CHRIST (Corpus Christi), June 6, 2021
***Second Reading* (Heb 9:11-15)**
Brothers and sisters: When Christ came as high priest of the good things that have come to be, passing through the greater and more perfect tabernacle not made by hands, that is, not belonging to this creation, he entered once for all into the sanctuary, not with the blood of goats and calves but with his own blood, thus obtaining eternal redemption. For if the blood of goats and bulls and the sprinkling of a heifer's ashes can sanctify those who are defiled so that their flesh is cleansed, how much more will the blood of Christ, who through the eternal Spirit offered himself unblemished to God, cleanse our consciences from dead works to worship the living God.

For this reason he is mediator of a new covenant: since a death has taken place for deliverance from transgressions under the first covenant, those who are called may receive the promised eternal inheritance.

THE ASSUMPTION OF THE BLESSED VIRGIN MARY, August 15, 2021

***Second Reading* (1 Cor 15:20-27)**

Brothers and sisters: Christ has been raised from the dead, the firstfruits of those who have fallen asleep. For since death came through man, the resurrection of the dead came also through man. For just as in Adam all die, so too in Christ shall all be brought to life, but each one in proper order: Christ the firstfruits; then, at his coming, those who belong to Christ; then comes the end, when he hands over the Kingdom to his God and Father, when he has destroyed every sovereignty and every authority and power. For he must reign until he has put all his enemies under his feet. The last enemy to be destroyed is death, for "he subjected everything under his feet."

ALL SAINTS, November 1, 2021

***Second Reading* (1 John 3:1-3)**

Beloved: See what love the Father has bestowed on us that we may be called the children of God. Yet so we are. The reason the world does not know us is that it did not know him. Beloved, we are God's children now; what we shall be has not yet been revealed. We do know that when it is revealed we shall be like him, for we shall see him as he is. Everyone who has this hope based on him makes himself pure, as he is pure.

OUR LORD JESUS CHRIST, KING OF THE UNIVERSE
November 21, 2021

***Second Reading* (Rev 1:5-8)**

Jesus Christ is the faithful witness, the firstborn of the dead and ruler of the kings of the earth. To him who loves us and has freed us from our sins by his blood, who has made us into a kingdom, priests for his God and Father, to him be glory and power forever and ever. Amen.

Behold, he is coming amid the clouds, / and every eye will see him, / even those who pierced him. / All the peoples of the earth will lament him. / Yes. Amen.

"I am the Alpha and the Omega," says the Lord God, "the one who is and who was and who is to come, the almighty."